MENTALLY AT WORK

ABOUT THE AUTHOR

From the start of her career as an Occupational Therapist, Genevieve Hawkins has had a passion for understanding and influencing the psychology of how people not just cope but thrive under pressure. This passion led her to further study in and exploration of how leaders, teams and cultures perform and has seen Genevieve shift from the health system to consulting to the Corporate world. Genevieve is now a senior executive with extensive experience in leading major change programs in large organisations and is cognisant of typically seeing things from a different perspective given her mix of experiences and qualifications. What she felt was missing in the market was practical, relatable and scalable guidance for senior leaders linking the trifecta of their own mental health, with the mental health of their team and the organisation's performance.

In an ever-changing, complex world, how we lead has become an increasingly critical skill. Genevieve hopes that this book can guide leaders to lead in a sustainable way for them, their teams and their businesses, so that we may collectively reverse the trend on mental illness in the developed world.

MENTALLY AT WORK

Optimising health and business
performance through connection

GENEVIEVE HAWKINS

First published in 2020 by Mentally at Work, Melbourne, Australia.

Book design: Ckaos
Printer: Ingram Spark, Australia

ISBN: 978-0-6483928-7-3

Disclaimer: The material throughout this publication is only representative of general comments, instead of professional advice. Its intention is not to provide specific guidance for any particular circumstances. It should not be relied upon for any decision to take action or not to take action on any matter which it covers. Readers should obtain professional advice wherever appropriate, and before making any such decision. To the maximum extent permitted by law, the author and publisher disclaim all responsibility and liability to any person, arising directly or indirectly from any person taking or not taking action based on the information in this book.

CONTENTS

Foreword VII

Preface IV

Introduction 1

CHAPTER ONE   The second half of the chessboard 9

CHAPTER TWO   Why mental health is a personal issue 22

CHAPTER THREE   The classroom and the shadow 53

CHAPTER FOUR   You cannot outsource mental health – it is your song 71

CHAPTER FIVE   Connecting to self 94

CHAPTER SIX   The currency of connection 126

CHAPTER SEVEN   From connection to curiosity to control – the magic formula 148

CHAPTER EIGHT   Crisis management 172

CHAPTER NINE   Is it sticky enough? 195

Epilogue 212

Your ready reckoner 215

Acknowledgements 217

FOREWORD

I fell into the mental health field and I fell into a friendship with Genevieve. We met through work and bonded over our shared passion for mental health at work.

Recent years have seen a seismic shift as leaders grasp the 'why' of mentally healthy workplaces and a workplace 'industry' has burgeoned. Today it's relatively rare for me to meet a business leader who subscribes still to the antiquated view that the mental health of their people is none of their business, or that they will never be affected by poor mental health.

If business leaders aren't thinking about the mental health of their workforce, they're losing money, productivity and brilliant people.

In a world that will be rebuilding through the aftershocks of COVID-19, this has never been truer.

But fruit bowls and yoga don't cut it. Implementing a mental health workplace strategy is not about ticking boxes or the feel good factor; it's about meaningful, measurable and ongoing structural, cultural and policy changes. Some businesses are doing better than others, and those who are doing it best have genuinely committed leaders who are prepared to show vulnerability and courage, to question the status quo and sit in what can be an uncomfortable space.

It has to start and end at the top and it always comes back to the skills and behaviours of each of us. And trust my amazing friend to write a book that addresses the very thing I know many leaders and managers are craving.

Like Genevieve, this is an open-hearted but cut-through guide. It lays out pragmatic tips and practical strategies. It's fun and challenging.

Your leadership will be better for this book and it will help you too because, as Genevieve writes: "Making someone else feel better each day helps your mental health as well as theirs."

Georgie Harman
CEO
Beyond Blue

PREFACE

I wrote this book before COVID-19 was identified, let alone a pandemic. I was in the final phase of editing when the pandemic hit Australia. It is fair to say that in those first turbulent weeks, I was incapable of doing anything further to progress the book. I was physically, emotionally, and mentally spent at the end of each day from my job. So drained, I don't know if I absorbed any of the TV I was watching to 'wind down'. But I also hit, as I suspect most authors do at this critical point, an incredible sense of vulnerability. Questions of whether the book was still relevant. What to do from a release date perspective, as my previous plans were no longer going to work in a world of social distancing. Did people have the capacity to absorb the material given the world's challenges? Had I done all this work for nothing?

So, I sat on it. And it weighed on me. And I watched the world. And here is what I saw. In a world where anxiety levels were already very high, it just went up another notch, or two, or three. The level of uncertainty that the world faced was taking its toll on everyone. Some were able to still step into this uncertainty and lead. Others were struggling to manage their anxiety, let alone lead others. The reality of our collective vulnerability was hitting home.

I have to thank my sister Leonie for pulling me out of this slump and challenging me to get a move on with getting the book published. I realised that despite the plethora of information out there on anxiety and depression during the pandemic, that a book linking personal mental health with the mental health of our team and the performance of our organisation was still missing and needed more than ever.

The prediction has been that the leadership skill set that is needed more than anything in a complex world is the ability to sit comfortably in complexity and uncertainty. To be able to hold those opposing views and influence others to problem-solve together. The pandemic is the current challenge in which this leadership skill is needed. It is stretching us in so many ways, but it is muscles we need to build because this pandemic is only one of many challenges we face.

I do hope that this book can in some way help you as a leader to build much-needed muscles in your mental health and the mental health of your teams so you can unlock performance and be the leaders this complex world of ours needs.

Genevieve

INTRODUCTION

Are there conversations that go round and round your mind? Do certain things rattle your confidence? Or are you frustrated with team members who do not seem to be as resilient anymore? Or will not open up, and talk about what is going on?

Do any of these scenarios sound familiar? These are common stories from senior managers who seek my advice on how to deal with the tsunami of mental health concerns. They may be concerned about their mental health but not wanting to acknowledge it, deflecting it to outside factors. Or they are frustrated with the impact on performance when the team is not resilient. They worry that they are expected to be a psychologist as well as a leader. They want to care, but what does care look like when they are under pressure to deliver results?

Approximately 45% of Australians aged 16–85 will experience a mental health condition over their lifetime. In any one year, 1 in 5 Australians will have experienced a common mental health condition—the most common being anxiety, depression and substance abuse disorder[*]. These rates are not unique to Australia. The World Health Organization now recognises depression as the number one cause of disability in the world with an 18.4% increase in diagnoses between 2005 and 2015[†]. While we don't have enough longitudinal data to understand how much the increased rate of diagnoses is due to more disclosure rather than an underlying increase in actual mental illness, these rate increases are occurring at a time in which we have increasing discord in our world, we are living through the impacts of a modern-day pandemic, and technology is expected to continue to disrupt the way that we live and work. I believe this is no coincidence.

The rapid changes in our world are inextricably linked with rates of mental illness.

In a world where, in theory, we are more connected than ever, we as individuals have never felt more disconnected. Nor have we felt more pressured to 'do more with less' in the perpetual search for growth in the economy. Then came a pandemic which has left so many feeling vulnerable and uncertain about our global future.

It is a big, complex issue, and our brains are complex machines. You may have experienced mental ill-health yourself and can appreciate the stigma that is still attached to it. You may have first-hand experiences with your own family and friends, or

---

[*] AIHW (2020). Mental Health Services in Australia, last updated 30 January 2020. Australian Institute of Health and Welfare. Australian Government.
[†] WHO Depression Fact Sheet Updated February 2017: Depression and other common mental disorders: global health estimates. Geneva. WHO.

with people within your team. You may have wondered whether someone's absences are due to mental illness, but no one wants to talk about it. You may have wondered whether a claim of mental ill-health was a way to avoid a performance discussion. If, as a senior leader, you are uncertain about what you can or should do in relation to your own and your team's mental health, but remain curious as to whether there is a solution that can unlock performance, then this book is for you.

While this is a big subject, over these next nine chapters, I want to help you see the connection between what you do and the collective mental health of your organisation. I will start by helping you understand why the complexity of the world is challenging for the human brain. I will then shift from macro to micro to help you better understand what is going on inside our brains that contribute to mental ill-health. I will then help you understand your impact as a leader both in one to one interaction and across a department or organisation. Once you understand this, we will explore what you can practically do for yourself, your relationships and the team environment to positively influence mental health. I will then leave you with some tips on dealing with particular challenges with mental ill-health and building the habits that will sustain you in this complex world we face.

Why me?

So why listen to me? While I am a senior manager who has led many major change programs and coached and developed many leaders and leadership teams over the years, it is the foundation of my health professional background and the up close and personal experiences, when combined with these change leadership positions, that enable me to provide you with a perspective that is practical, direct and useful to senior managers.

I started my working life post university as an occupational therapist, working with year 12 students managing stress pre-exams through my own business, and working in the health system in Australia and internationally, helping adults return to occupations, whether that was recovering from road trauma, open heart surgery, head injuries or other complex illnesses and injuries. My focus shifted almost 25 years ago to both physical injuries and psychological illness occurring in the workplace. This work took me through a variety of consulting and big business roles with further studies in occupational hazard management, organisational change management and business management. Through these roles, I have been fascinated with how people recover—or do not—from life's setbacks and what role the workplace, and the leader in that workplace, play in that recovery. From here, I expanded my focus to include understanding the role that the leader plays in optimum workplace performance, not just recovery.

Life, of course, throws you curveballs and I have had my fair share of these. From losing my father to cancer when I was in my mid-twenties, to experiencing the confusion and grief associated with the suicide of a friend, then a valued team member. I have also worked in unhealthy 'team' environments that contributed to me wobbling on the edge of burnout followed by losing a close friend to cancer. My determination to look after my mental health after facing significant challenges led me to push the boundaries in what I was reading and then testing in the workplace to find practical tools to which senior managers could relate. I realised how much my health background has helped me in leading and supporting others. In a world with increasing rates of mental illness being diagnosed, I have become passionate about helping to reverse the trend of mental illness in the developed world. Of course, I cannot do it alone, and this is where you come in. If you want to be a successful leader in this complex and uncertain 21st century, then you need to be able to understand and influence mental health.

The term 'mental health' has become popular over the last few years. I have seen an increase in the number of businesses promoting their mental health programs with 'mindfulness' and 'resilience' almost as popular terms as 'strategy' in business. There are countless books on individual aspects of mental health or trying to explain the medical background of mental illness. Separately there are books on leadership. But they rarely address the leader's impact on mental health per se. The challenge is finding a clear, simple guide on what to do as a manager to effectively lead when there are increased rates of disclosed mental illness. Even though I have always had an interest in mental health, and I am an avid reader, I would often pick up a self-development or health book and not feel connected to the language. I found that these books sat in one of two extremes. They were either medically oriented and valuable for clinicians in understanding the medical side in far more detail but would lose the business reader. Or they were 'new age' and not written in an accessible language for people wanting to understand what to do during a challenge or when time-poor. Drawing on my experiences as a health professional, line manager, change agent and mentor and coach, I have therefore shaped this book with a pragmatic language balanced between science and management action.

This book is not about implementing a 'mental wellbeing' program, nor is it a medical book. Rather, this book helps you to understand the basic medical foundation for mental health and ill-health; the role everyone plays individually; and the role you can play in how you lead to have a positive impact on others' mental health, not just avoid having a negative impact.

Given the external environment that we are facing, we as leaders need to take a more significant role in understanding mental health, and how our mental health (or mental ill-health) affects both us and others in the workplace.

We can no longer see this as someone else's responsibility or an individual problem; but instead, need to appreciate the influence we can have as role models and as shapers of culture and connection in the workplace.

It is about how you, as a leader, shape every day of the week and the future of your organisation and career. We must find a balance here. It is not helpful for individual recovery to blame a work environment for their ill health even though it may have contributed. Everyone needs to understand and own their health. But we can't just focus on the individual actions and ignore the shadow we cast as leaders. This is our opportunity to lead more effectively.

———

Why you?

If you have not yet been the almost one in two people who will experience some form of mental ill-health in their lifetime, you may think yourself immune. That your resilience and determination, that has got you to a senior level will get you through. Think again. As a senior manager, you are likely to be aware of the value of looking after your physical health. While you may not always get the amount of sleep you want, you are likely to have some form of physical exercise that helps you clear your head and not feel too guilty about what you might drink or eat.

But not enough senior managers understand the vulnerability that exists should they not take conscious steps to look after their mental health. The one thing that may have rattled you is the COVID-19 pandemic. If there is one benefit you can gain from this enormous global challenge, it is an appreciation of your vulnerability. You need to understand what it takes to look after your mental health, as much as your physical health to lead effectively. This is not something that happens to other people and not you. This is something that we all must own. As a senior leader, you have a greater responsibility, given the influence you have over the people with whom you interact. People look to you as a role model whether you like it or not. If you do not consistently set an example of how you look after your mental health, then you cannot reasonably expect your team to do this consistently. And that leaves performance wanting.

The property barons shout 'location, location, location!' Location is more important than any other factor in making money in property. I shout 'connection, connection, connection!'

Whether you like it or not, humans are social creatures. Our rapidly changing world is causing disconnection, and this is impacting performance. But connection is the most important factor in our mental health. Connection to ourselves and connection to others. Connection to a purpose at work and how we contribute to this. Connection to learning.

If you can understand how your brain operates independent of your conscious thought, you are in the best place to take active steps to not just look after your mental health but to help others in your organisation do so too. In our complex world, where we cannot know the challenges ahead, let alone the solutions, this skill set is invaluable.

———

What is coming up?

Reading this book, you will walk away with:

- An understanding of why looking after your mental health matters more today than it has ever mattered as we face a changing world.
- A practical understanding of the science behind your mental health and why you are not exempt regardless of your history to date.
- Some simple tools to look after your mental health.
- An understanding of why connection at work matters and how you cast shadows that, for better or worse, will affect what goes on for both your relationships and your team performance.
- How you, as a leader, can get better at connecting in the workplace and guide your team to build a mentally healthy workplace with detailed, useful but also practical and easy strategies to apply as a leader.

Leadership growth is made up of multiple 'ah-ha' moments. By reading this book, I hope that you can experience one or two of your own 'ah ha' moments. Through this growth, you can help me in reversing the trend of mental illness in the developed world by becoming a better version of yourself and leading others to do the same. This sets you up for a sustainable career as a leader in our complex world. Ready to learn? Then read on.

CHAPTER ONE

THE SECOND HALF OF THE CHESSBOARD

Have you heard the story of the peasant and the chessboard used to explain exponential growth[*]?

A very bright peasant invented the game of chess. He brought his game to the king to show him. The king was enthralled and said to the peasant, 'To pay you for creating this magnificent game, I will give you any reward you desire'.

The peasant said to him, 'I would like one grain of rice for the first square on that chessboard and then double the number of grains for each square following'.

The king looked at the peasant and protested. 'That is not enough', he proclaimed. But the peasant insisted, and the king agreed to pay him in grains of rice.

---

[*] The mathematician Ray Kurzweil is attributed as the original teller of this story. www.jupiterjenkins.com/the-second-half-of-the-chessboard

A week went by, and the peasant had still not received the rice owed to him. The king called in his advisors and asked, 'What has happened? Why haven't we given this rice to the peasant?' They said, 'Because we cannot afford it. We do not have that much rice!'. The king was astonished! But what the king failed to understand was the concept of exponential growth.

At two squares, the king's payment is only two grains of rice and at three squares, four grains of rice. At the end of the first line, it is only 128 grains of rice. It doesn't seem like much, does it?

By the end of the third line of the chessboard; the payment is at 8.39 million grains of rice. By the time you hit the second half of the chessboard the rate of growth accelerates beyond comprehension. By the final square on the board, the payment is more rice than the kingdom could possibly grow.

That is exponential growth. The rapid rate of change in the way we work and by extension, live—and that is what we face right now in the modern world—the second half of the chessboard.

FIGURE ONE

The exponential growth curve

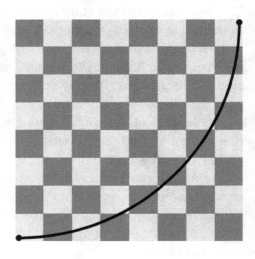

This simple story of how hard it is to grasp the impact of exponential growth was told to me by Michael Priddis, founder and CEO of Faethm. His boutique consultancy company assists organisations and governments in adapting to our fourth industrial revolution. Disruptive technology is exponentially changing the way we live and work—the beginning of the second half of the chessboard.

We cannot even begin to imagine what these changes will bring. But we have glimpsed the concept of exponential growth, watching what felt like a sudden increase in the number of infections during the 2019/20 COVID-19 pandemic. There was little global appreciation in the very early days of this pandemic, how quickly the infections would increase. We were in the first line or two of the chessboard. Then the rates of infection went from tens of thousands to well beyond a million in a relatively short space of time. The pandemic has demonstrated not only how quickly rates of infection increase but also how quickly technology adapts to meet needs.

The exponential growth of technology, which has then been turbo-charged by the COVID-19 pandemic, is shaping a new future of work. There are opportunities as well as complex challenges in this future. What industries and jobs will evolve, appear or disappear? How will technology speed up recovery? When will the next plateau in the rate of change be? As leaders, we want to harness these changes. We want to make the most of the opportunities coming our way. But our brains can struggle to adapt to the speed of information.

Rapid change means it is critical to get the right strategy in place now for your mental health and the collective mental health of your teams.

Change is about performance—not just now, but deep into the second half of the chessboard. You need only look at the rapid impact of the COVID-19 pandemic and how quickly businesses and governments have had to respond. Are you fully prepared?

———

What is the link between mental health and the second half of the chessboard?

I believe the exponential growth in change, and therefore, the complexity we face is contributing to the increased rates of mental ill-health in the western world, now and into the future. While some may argue the increased rate of diagnosis is the result of less stigma leading to increased disclosure, the frequency of diagnosis of children at primary and secondary school age would suggest there are also other factors at play. Hugh van Cuylenburg, a teacher and founder of The Resilience Project[*], teaches children across Australia about the importance of their mental health. He reports that kids are now bombarded with the same volume of information within one week, that adults received in a year as kids. The speed and amount of information we consume is increasing exponentially. He also reports that 25% of primary and 40% of secondary school students in Australia have been diagnosed with some form of mild mental illness. These stats were quoted before the COVID-19 pandemic hit the world then the level of anxiety across the globe became palpable. There is perhaps now greater acceptance of what uncertainty can do to everyone's mental health.

While you may think that you are healthy and resilient right now having achieved a senior role, the exponential pace of change is placing strain on everyone's brain, including yours. If

[*] www.theresilienceproject.com.au – an organisation delivering programs and evidence-based strategies to build resilience.

our kids are showing signs of struggling to cope—and their minds are more malleable than ours—there are serious implications for adults. You may not even realise how much your mind and body is already under stress. In my mentoring role, with multi-layers of leaders across organisations, I see many managers who feel overwhelmed, exhausted and challenged by the pace of change and its impact on them and their teams. Yet we are only at the cusp of the second half of this chessboard. You do not want to be like the proverbial frog sitting happily in the heating water, slowly warming up, oblivious to impact on life until it is too late. You need to acknowledge that the water is heating up around you in the business world and start adapting now before the temperature gets too hot to reverse its impact.

It is not just your brain that must adapt to the speed of change, but your teams' collective mindset. We are not dealing with a straightforward 'survival of the fittest' where you can just recruit those who 'can cope'. There just will not be enough of 'them'. We need to lead our organisations in learning how to strengthen the way our brains process what is happening. Your ability to get your mind to adapt and help guide the collective adaptation of your teams' mindset to these changes will make the difference—the difference to your success individually, your teams' health and your organisation's performance.

What is needed for leadership success in the second half of the chessboard?

Homo Sapiens are tribal. Feeling like we belong to a tribe brings psychological safety. We perform at our best when we feel psychologically safe. Without being consciously aware of it, our brains seek this safety.

The current level of change and uncertainty in the world, however, is causing people to feel worried or threatened. This 'threat' results in people looking for the 'tribe' in which they feel the safest. One of the quickest ways to feel like you belong is finding others that share the same view as you, inside or outside work. There is safety in belonging to a tribe and having other people rally around the same outlook, often resulting in feeling passionately 'right' about a particular view. Of course, being 'right' means others have to be wrong. This tribalism is why we see increasingly polarising views. The "I am right, and you are wrong" and "That what I say is true and what you say is false".

When we are uncertain, we hunt to find our tribe—to find 'safety'. There is no coincidence that these sometimes illogical, often un-reasoned and almost always polarised views, are increasing in intensity with the increased diagnoses of mental illness. Our collective brains are seeking out safety and then feeling more threatened when the 'other side' increases their intensity of 'rightness'. It becomes a battle of who can argue louder and is a vicious cycle. The polarisation of thinking and tribalism does not enable practical problem solving, which we need in our complex changing world, let alone create the sustainable psychological safety our brains need to perform. We cannot achieve when we are feeling threatened. We are too busy protecting ourselves. We need to do something differently, both individually and collectively, if we are going to arrest the growing trend of mental illness in the developed world and achieve the business outcomes we want.

If as a leader, you do not adapt, then you will not be able to maximise the opportunities that the second half of the chessboard offers us.

In considering the second half of the chessboard and current discord, the question then becomes 'What are the skills that are most needed?' We have difficulty imagining what jobs will exist in the future because we are unsure what technology and a post-COVID-19 pandemic world will bring. But it's essential to understand the leadership skills that set us up for the best path for that future.

Deloitte* identifies that 'soft' skills, rather than harder technical skills, are far more significant in this future world given its uncertainty. In particular, the ability to communicate with others and to understand how to approach complex problem-solving. My experience tells me there is a direct link between these skill requirements for performance, your mental health and the collective mental health of your teams.

At the heart of these skills, is the ability to wield the power of connection. Connection is about understanding what you and your teams need and creating the psychologically safe environment where your teams can perform at their best. It is creating a much bigger 'tribe' in your organisation, built on trust and common purpose, not fear or a 'We are right, they're wrong' mentality. This type of connection with a team delivers performance and will get you thriving in the second half of the chessboard. If you cannot master how to connect with others, not only will your career suffer, but your mental health will too. Connection is the key to the second half of the chessboard.

---

* The Future of Work. Deloitte White Paper 2019.

What does connection look like in this complex world?

I had the unique experience of running a similar change program twice in the same organisation, which very few people get to do. The first time around I was relatively new to a senior role and made the fatal mistake of many a leader, walking in and thinking, 'Blind Freddy can see what the problem and solution is.' Therefore, I followed the well-trodden path of painting what you believe is a great vision of the future and did the whole 'you are either on the bus, or you are not' as part of the change. This vision fell on deaf ears for some of my team as they couldn't see the need for change. We eventually got where we needed to go, but it was an incredibly slow and painful process. It's fair to say that I lost some good people along the way because they became disengaged with how things were running. But clearly, I did a half-decent job because I got invited back to achieve this same change program in a different location.

I took a very different approach the second time around. Interestingly, the second group faced the same challenges as the first. I knew the desired outcome was going to be essentially the same. Still, I appreciated that what I needed to do for the fastest and the most sustainable way forward was to be able to connect with the team and get them to trust me—then inspire them to generate the change that was needed.

There is a real difference in how a team can operate when you are the connection and glue that inspires them to drive themselves, compared to when you are the manager pulling them all along. The second time around, while slower to start, ultimately evolved much faster and with fewer casualties and more significant longer-term financial results. I learnt the hard way how vital connection with others is for long-term sustainable results where the whole team performs because they're all passionate about the outcome. This learning was some time ago. Sands have shifted. The demand for connection is higher than ever, given the uncertainty we face.

While the term connection may sound 'fluffy' to you, I am not going to talk about this in a fluffy way as I believe this is why senior leaders often disconnect from genuinely understanding the hidden opportunity of connection. I am going to explain the science in a practical way that will enhance your performance as a leader to help you achieve the results you want for the long game. Regardless of where your experiences place you to date, you need to recognise that science confirms that our brains crave connection.

Real connection enhances performance.

In the second half of the chessboard, the need for that connection is even more compelling. Technology continues to make it easier for people to identify alternative ways of building careers. If you want to attract the talent you need and keep the whole team reliably performing—connection is the key. Regardless of where your passions and interests lie, your teams aren't going to achieve long term if you do not grasp the science of connection. How you lead has to adapt to this second half.

Connection in a complex world for our teams is:
- **I am known.** Manager and team alike understand the background and current situation for others in the team.
- **I am valued** for the skills I bring to the table, and I appreciate the skills of those around me to solve whatever problems we may face.
- **I can voice a different view** without being concerned about how I am viewed; indeed, I love expressing a different opin-

ion as we can then debate the perspectives better and my voice is heard equally with others around the table. I still feel safe with a different view.

- **I am aware** of my own emotions and feel comfortable sharing my vulnerability with others in the team, as I know that all I will ever get is support.
- **I can laugh** and make others laugh in the team.
- **I am inspired** by my vulnerable leader to keep wanting to push forward and solve problems together.

Connection causes a positive chemical reaction in the brain when we feel it. Likewise, disconnection causes an adverse chemical reaction. Connection directly influences performance. When your team feel connected, they will become high performers able to collectively solve the complex problems of the second half of the chessboard. If they do not, they will not.

It is only through your direct team experiencing a connection with you, that you have a hope of influencing it throughout the organisation/department. In creating connections, you are achieving three things at once. It improves your mental health, your team's mental health and delivers performance—the triple whammy.

However, you cannot effectively connect to others unless you can connect with and understand yourself. For the team to start to feel connected to you, they need to see you as more than just the senior manager. They need to see a little bit of the human behind the façade, and understanding your strengths and struggles is their starting point. Without this insight, you will struggle to connect. Enabling your team to see a little bit of you becomes a foundation block of connection.

———

Where are you now?

Let's start with the principle of understanding yourself a bit first.

Before you head into Chapter Two, it is worth reflecting on these questions:
- What is currently causing you restless nights?
- What conversations are you replaying in your mind?
- What is rattling your confidence?
- What is worrying you?
- What is frustrating or annoying you?
- Where is your reaction disproportionate to what is going on?

Note the answers to these questions down so you can use them as you reflect on how the brain processes information in Chapter Two.

There is a risk of thinking, 'I am fine. I know what I am doing. I am getting everything under control. It's just my team or organisation I need to worry about.' If you have got anything out of this chapter, I do hope it is that the pace of change will be beyond our imagining in the second half of the chessboard. You may think you are fine, but the reality is that everyone struggles in some way with what they face in life and work. Putting up a façade of full strength does not build a connection. Yet connection is the key to future performance.

How do you then assess where your skills of connection lie? What are your assumptions? What data are you using to inform you that you are good at 'connecting'? In HR terms, connection in some ways has been taken over by the concept of engagement. Therefore, when the question is raised regarding connection, you may think about how engaged the team is and turn to HR to give data from engagement surveys or 360-degree reviews or exit interviews. If your first instinct is to go to this data, it's a reasonable starting point. Always remember the adage—"lies, damn lies and then there are statistics". The best business decisions come from a range of data sets—hard and fast current data but also experience that brings gut instinct. Engagement surveys alone are not enough to test connection. Understanding the strength of the underlying connection with the team needs to be both data and gut-driven.

Realistically you cannot personally connect with teams of teams in the same way. You can, however, 'role model' building a connection with your senior team. Thereby setting expectations for what they do for the next layer down and so on through the organisation.

Can you answer these questions about your direct reports?
- What are their fears?
- When was the last time they confided in you about something with which they were struggling?
- What was the last thing you did to truly show them that you understood and supported them in what they were doing?
- When was the last time you sought their advice about an issue with which you were grappling?
- How have you helped the person who frustrates you the most to have confidence in themselves?
- What are you consciously doing to inspire your team around purpose?
- What are you consciously doing to stop and listen to their concerns and collaboratively find solutions?
- How capable are each of your direct reports in doing this for their teams?

Think about the answers to those questions, along with engagement surveys or other data. What does this data tell you about how good you are at connecting? The risk at a senior level is the perception that the overall strategy is the more exciting and significant part of the role. Team engagement can often be considered an abstract concept led by HR and others. But if you build connection as a senior leadership team, it is incredible what can be achieved. And if you do not, the second half of the chessboard will leave you behind.

Key things to remember

- The fourth industrial revolution is upon us. The "second half of the chessboard" will see exponential growth in technology and therefore exponential growth of change in the way we live and work, for better and worse.
- We cannot be sure what is around the corner.
- The human brain is **already** struggling to adapt to the rate of information exchange, contributing to the diagnoses of mental illness in the western world.
- The pace of change and impact on the human brain brings complexity that needs a different leader.
- At the heart of this different leader is the ability to connect.
- The ability to connect and understand self, to then connect with others and stay curious to the complex world we have is the skill set you need to future proof your career and have an impact.

We do not know what we are facing in the future. Still, if you can truly work out how to leverage connection positively, then you will be future-proofing your leadership career. You will be able to contribute significant value along the way, not just to your organisation, but to society, in helping to arrest the trend of increasing mental illness. Increasing world complexity will make this difficult but the opportunity is enormous. So, leap and reap the rewards.

CHAPTER TWO

WHY MENTAL HEALTH IS A PERSONAL ISSUE

How physically fit are you? If you are surviving at a senior management level, you will likely be able to describe your physical fitness accurately. But how would you describe your mental fitness?

In the last chapter, we discussed the environmental—or macro—perspective. This discussion should have you thinking about what is needed for the second half of the chessboard. Now it's time to delve into what is happening at the micro, or individual level, to strengthen your mental health to enable ongoing high performance.

In this chapter, I will explain a little bit more about what mental health is all about and introduce the connection between your mental health and business performance—enabling you to perform now and into the future.

The expectation is that we are likely to see increased diagnoses of mental ill-health conditions across the world. Truly understanding mental health and the link between collective mental health and performance will future proof your career as a senior manager.

I want to start by introducing you to the concept of the continuum of mental health*. Then we will explore why you can move up and down this continuum based on what is happening with the chemicals in your brain. We will then talk about what will help you maintain or get back to peak mental health to deliver and perform consistently.

———

What is the continuum of mental health?

We all understand that if we eat doughnuts or smoke cigarettes every day, at some point, it will come back to bite us. Our education through school and home and what we see in the media make us aware that sleep, exercise and a good diet are critical to our physical health. It appears though that we do not all understand what is needed to maintain our mental health. When I asked you earlier about how mentally fit you think you are, I wonder whether, like many senior managers I have coached, you automatically thought "I am fine. I am mentally tough." Typically, this thought process comes from an absence of personal experience of mental illness,

---

* I was first introduced to this continuum concept by my psychiatry lecturer in 1989 and then added the concept of the physical continuum and the colours as a way of better explaining this during my consulting career. I have since identified that the Mental Health Commission of Canada has also utilised a continuum of these colours to explain Mental Health and help first responders in understanding and coping with mental ill health. While I have not used their information for the purposes of this book, their website, theworkingmind.ca is valuable for additional resources on responding to mental ill health.

compared to awareness of what you consciously do to maintain mental health the way you would maintain physical health.

I vividly recall sitting next to a friend in a first-year psychiatry lecture years ago. As the lecturer described some of the symptoms of mental illnesses, I recognised some of my behaviours, thoughts and feelings, as did my friend. After about 20 minutes, we had diagnosed ourselves as having about ten different mental illnesses. The lecturer was deliberately provocative in attempting to get us to understand this concept of the continuum of mental health. Poor mental health is not about a diagnosis per se nor the feelings, but critically the impact on daily living that identifies the difference between suffering from a mental illness and merely having a bad day, week or month.

An individual's health shown as a colour scale continuum going from green through yellow, orange and ultimately to red explains this concept better. This continuum exists for both physical and mental health, summarised in Figure Two and Three on the following pages. It is useful to start with the more comfortable space of physical health to help you understand how this works.

If I am 'green'—I am sleeping and eating well, I have some form of exercise that I am doing, and I feel reasonably okay. It is the balance of these key factors, that largely influence how physically healthy we are. It is not necessary to be a super athlete to be in the green zone. Most of us can happily exist in green with our physical health.

All of us, at some stage, will have had rough patches. That rough patch could be drinking too much alcohol, or not getting enough sleep due to stress from an impending deadline or being unwell with a head cold. We have all had those days or weeks in which we do not feel great. That is sliding into 'yellow'. If we recognise that we do not feel that great, most of us will then choose a response that will get us back on track to perform reasonably quickly. It could be an early night, a 'no-sugar' day, an extra walk/run in the

The continuum of physical health

THE PHYSICAL HEALTH CONTINUUM

GREEN	YELLOW	ORANGE	RED
Consistent balanced diet	Not eating well	Consistent unbalanced diet	Severe physical illness needing clinical care to improve/manage
Regular exercise	Not exercising for a short period	Overweight and/or very unfit – breathless in day to day activities	Ability to reliably hold down full-time work and perform is compromised either short term or long term
Sleeping well	Restless nights without sleeping		
Reasonably good energy levels	Binge eating or heavy drinking	Minor injuries – a muscle tear, continually ill with minor issues	
	Obsessing about diets		Treatment starts outside the inpatient stay but at the seriously dark red end, people are hospitalised and ultimately the darkest of the red is life threatening

GREEN	YELLOW	ORANGE	RED

fresh air. It takes us back to green. If we stay in the yellow for too long, however, we can start shifting into 'orange'.

Orange is not so healthy. We might be a bit overweight, not sleeping well, regularly catching colds/flu, tearing a calf muscle, or just struggling to physically manage. We might need a bit of outside help to get us back on track, perhaps seeking the expertise of a qualified health professional, such as a physiotherapist or dietician. But we are not yet at that serious illness level. Just a level in which some form of external help is valuable to get us back to being able to perform the way we want to. If, however, we slide into the red, we have a serious physical illness that needs medical attention because of the impact on daily living.

We can all shift up and down on this continuum. Sometimes, because of the roll of the genetic dice, we land in red for specific illnesses right from the outset, or we are at least at higher risk for a particular medical condition. For example, a history of coronary artery disease in your family will place you at a higher risk of landing into the red with a heart attack. However, even with a diagnosed physical illness, it can be controlled in a way that you remain at the green end of the continuum.

This is exactly the same for our mental health. What I find frustrating is when the term 'mental health' is misused instead of 'mental illness'.

'Mental health' is not something that happens to someone who is not as resilient or as tough as you. A mental 'illness' is what happens when someone isn't looking after their mental health, or perhaps genetics and environmental factors combine in a way which impacts their daily living. Just like with a physical illness, it is not the diagnosis itself, but the impact on everyday life that slides us down the continuum. There is a greater understanding of the difference between physical health and physical illness but less so between mental health and mental illness. The reality is that we all have to look after our mental health as much as our physical health.

FIGURE THREE

The continuum of psychological health

THE PSYCHOLOGICAL HEALTH CONTINUUM

GREEN	YELLOW	ORANGE	RED
A range of good emotions but overall feeling balanced and broadly in control	Feeling unbalanced /flat or frustrated, annoyed, irritated	Weeks of persistent flat or down moods that are starting to interfere with relationships	Severe mental illness needing clinical care to improve/manage
Experiencing joy and happiness at times but also contentment and high engagement	Angry beyond the actual conversation	Mild anxiety – heart palpitations	The ability to reliably hold down full-time work and perform is compromised either short term or long term
Feel like you belong	Not sleeping well, not eating well, not exercising	Worried most of the time about a range of issues	Treatment starts outside the inpatient stay but at the seriously dark red end, people are hospitalised and ultimately the darkest of the red is life threatening
	Can't stop thinking about a particular issue	Allowing emotions to dictate responses to situations with responses out of proportion to actual events	

| GREEN | YELLOW | ORANGE | RED |

The first thing to accept about this continuum, is that no-one sits permanently in the green space. At a minimum, we all regularly move between green and yellow. Many people would like to think that 'mental health' is someone else's problem and they are fine. We are all vulnerable. We have all had those times which have caused us to feel a bit uncomfortable, we have had arguments with people or difficult conversations at work and we find ourselves feeling particularly irritated, angry, frustrated or not sleeping. These emotions and the subsequent effect on our concentration, sleep, eating, or diet patterns moves us into the yellow space.

If we identify that we have shifted, we can act to move back to green reasonably quickly. Again, as a senior manager you will have been faced with pressures over an extended period and usually have some techniques, often sub-conscious, that move you back to green. But if you do not keep arming yourself with different methods to get you back to full green, you can get stuck. Without realising it, your yellow becomes 'the new green', and then you risk a slow deterioration into orange. Just like that frog in that slowing warming water.

Similar to not exercising for an extended period, your body adjusts. You do not see any change day-to-day, but slowly your weight increases and your heart is de-conditioned. In the orange space of physical health, you seek some additional assistance from others to get you back on track. So too, in the mental health space, where an executive coach, a psychologist, or other experts in this area can help guide you back before you get to the red zone of serious mental illnesses impacting your daily living.

As with our physical health, family history and the roll of the genetic dice could mean we are in the red of mental illness from an early age. Or a trauma, again the same as physical health, suddenly lands us in the red. If that roll of the dice places some-

PRACTICAL STEPS:

Increasing awareness of your position on the continuum

Think about this concept of the Mental Health Continuum from green, to yellow, to orange, to red. Keep a journal over a week of how you are feeling. At the end of each day, ask yourself the following questions:

- How have I felt throughout this day?

- Has it been a good, significant, solid day?

- Has it been a day that has been a bit shaky, sitting firmly in yellow?

- Have negative feelings persisted throughout the week? What is triggering this?

- What am I actively doing to bring myself back to green?

one there, they need qualified professional help to bring them back along the continuum, which is not the purpose of this book to explain. If you recognise from these descriptions that you are close to red and facing a crisis, please call the relevant support line in your country[*] and get help straight away.

This book is about you consciously managing the movement between green and orange. Then guiding your team on this same continuum. Stop and take a moment or two to study the two continuums and consider where you currently are.

We are all vulnerable to mental illness the same as we are susceptible to physical illness if we do not consciously choose to do the right things to protect our health.

---

[*] If you are in Australia, please call Lifeline on 13 11 14.

Have you seen the movie *Inside Out*? For those of you who haven't, it follows a pre-teen girl and a range of different characters that "exist" inside her brain, representing her various emotions. These characters have conversations with each other about what she is experiencing. In any one of these conversations, one character (emotion) becomes the 'winner', influencing her behaviour, which her parents are finding increasingly difficult to predict. This emotional shifting is an excellent example of how someone can move up and down the Mental Health Continuum.

It is helpful to know that we all have 'conversations' going on in our head like this (you are not the only one). Sometimes those 'conversations' are replaying an interaction with someone or rehearsing a new one. Other conversations we have are with ourselves. Many of these conversations will happen at a subconscious level of the brain. When these conversations make sense of the world, we sit in the green. When these conversations become more focused on what is not quite right, we start to slip into yellow. This is the classroom inside your head

Can you learn to speak this language?

The continuum, with its sliding scale from green to red is valuable because it gives us a language to break down the stigma of talking about our mental health. We do not tend to hesitate to say we are not feeling great physically—"I did not sleep well; I am a bit stiff and sore; I have an upset stomach." We are not so good at saying "I am flat, anxious, struggling mentally." Being able to say, "I am a bit in yellow at the moment," is enough to start a conversation on whether space or support is the next best action. Critical to this though is accepting that you are just as vulnerable as the next person to being mentally unwell. The same as you are vulnerable to being physically unwell.

What is going on inside my head that influences where I am on the continuum?

Our mental health has multiple contributors. Our genetic make-up, our experiences, and how our brain processes situations based on events in our life to date.

You might like to think, as an evolved human, that you are entirely in control of your brain, your thoughts, your emotions. Think again. The classroom inside your head can be unruly at times. It can also be somewhat illogical but with good intent.

Let's talk about the animal brain versus the executive brain (the subcortex versus the cortex).

You do not actively think about breathing or digestion; your brain knows what to do, and it directs the body to do it automatically. For ease of explanation, this is our animal brain at work—geared for our survival. Just like a tree 'knows' how to grow. Our animal brain 'knows' how to keep us alive. You aren't consciously telling the animal brain to sleep, breathe, digest, or sweat. It is a smart computer in its own right. It operates independently of our conscious thought to keep us alive.

Our animal brain is hard-wired for survival. It influences our thinking for better or worse by triggering four fascinating 'chemicals' or messengers. Learning how these messengers operate helps you better change your focus and thinking and, ultimately, performance. It is important to note that there is much about how our brains work that we still do not understand. Researchers keep making discoveries and gain new insights. But let's try to help you understand some key facts that we do know about four mighty messengers in the brain that are seeking to find the right balance for survival. This knowledge will help you make conscious choices to keep getting back to green. Understanding these four chemicals and how you can consciously influence them helps you keep moving back to green and maximising the time you stay in green. Master these, and your life will change for the better.

Cortisol

Our animal brains are continually scanning the environment for threat. They are hard-wired for this. If we are feeling stressed in some way, our animal brain recognises we are vulnerable, that we are not at the top of our game, which it considers a threat and, in response, releases cortisol. It increases our alertness and is essentially signalling, 'there is a threat—how do I respond to this threat?' It's not a bad thing if it's only a small amount for a short time. In early Neolithic time, when you could be eaten if you weren't always alert to potential threats, this constant scanning makes sense. In the developed world, a significant proportion of the population does not have to worry about where they are going to sleep, or where they will get their next meal. We have got those covered, but our brain keeps scanning for threats. It wants to ensure our survival. Interestingly, our minds struggle to tell the difference between a physical and a psychological threat. Either way, a perceived 'threat' triggers the release of cortisol, the body's 'stress' messenger, which increases our alertness. This alertness helps enable us to make decisions to get ourselves out of danger.

When we take action to remove ourselves from danger we counteract the cortisol effect and reassure the brain that everything is okay. The cortisol release ceases. But if we do not take those actions quickly and refocus, cortisol keeps surging through our body.

This can shift us into yellow, and then into orange if we do not take appropriate steps. Sometimes this happens so gradually we do not realise. The constant high pressure at senior manager level without counterbalance can land managers in the orange (or even red) zone.

The good news is that there are three 'chemicals' or messengers in our animal brain that can counterbalance cortisol. If we can consciously choose actions that trigger these, they balance out the cortisol and get us back to green.

Oxytocin

Some people call oxytocin 'the happy drug'. Oxytocin is the chemical of connection. When we feel like we belong, oxytocin release is the driver. From when homo sapiens first walked the earth, there has always been safety in numbers. We are tribal by nature. If we woke up in the cave and found that everyone had left, cortisol would flood the brain. It is a threat to be alone as it is harder to survive that way. Who knows what wild animal is around the corner? When there was a taking of turns to sleep or stay on sentry duty, the animal brain would trigger oxytocin. It knows that being with others who can help protect the group equals greater safety. We are fundamentally hard-wired for this connection. Connection means safety. Safety means survival.

We need 'our tribe'. This connection to 'our tribe'
keeps us alive.

Oxytocin is released when we feel more connected and helps keep us in, or shift us toward, the green zone on the continuum as it makes us feel good.

Serotonin

Serotonin is about the value that you bring to 'this tribe'. It's that sense of strength that comes from being recognised for what you 'bring to the table'. If I am the one with the spear that killed the bear and everyone is celebrating what I did, then I am going to feel the effects of that serotonin. It's the same when we think about it in the modern work context. We have delivered these amazing results, people are saying, 'Well done, that is fantastic,' and it feels awesome. That is the serotonin coming through for us. For Neolithic humans, you can imagine it was an increased sense of security in being able to remain in the pack, knowing you're valued for a particular skill. Our animal brain sees it the same way in our modern world.

When we feel valued for a skill set that we have, it increases our sense of connection to others. Feeling valued makes us feel connected. Feeling connected gets us back to green.

Dopamine

We are hard-wired to seek patterns as much as we are hard-wired for connection. Dopamine plays an interesting role in this. It is the drug of reward or pleasure. It can be addictive, but wise choices help you maximise its benefit. Our brains cannot consciously process everything that is coming at our senses every day. Our animal brains learn to recognise patterns so information can be 'clumped' and the brain can go back to scanning for other threats—Making it much easier to help make sense of the world around us. We can filter out noise or physical incursion in our environment as our animal brain has learnt they aren't a threat. Our executive brain does not keep describing to us every colour our eyes see or every sound our ears here. The animal brain 'knows' what information it has clumped and therefore, is no longer a worry. It 'knows' the people who have our backs, who will look after us. Our brains like predictability. Predictability reassures the animal brain. It makes the animal brain feel safer. Our animal brain is also curious. It wants to understand the world in which it operates. It likes it when it finds a pattern. When it identifies a pattern that enables a 'clumping' it means there is less to process in the world—this triggers dopamine.

Dopamine is also known as the pleasure drug. When we do something that makes us feel good, our brain remembers it. The mind wants to experience it again. This pattern-seeking brain is curious. It likes it when we set a task, then we achieve it, and we get the same good feeling—this triggers dopamine. It is a reward to the brain. It builds a habit. But if we keep repeating the same thing, it will not keep triggering the same level of dopamine. It feels great when we get a dopamine hit, and our brain wants more, the risk is losing the balance in what we do. If we can stay curious and keep learning and achieving new things, and we feel connected and valued, we can keep getting healthy doses of dopamine which is balanced by the oxytocin and serotonin. If we think life is ordinary and flat most of the time, then we may seek out a high-risk activity, potentially leading to a big rush of dopamine. This temporary high comes at a risk.

*If we cannot find the right balance in our day to day lives,
then we keep hunting for bigger and bigger highs.*

Hunting for more significant highs can drive us on as leaders to make more money, take on more significant challenges. Like cortisol, this is not a bad thing. But it comes at the cost of our long-term mental health if we do not learn to find the balance in everyday life to manage it. We risk the thought process of 'I'll be happy when... I make millions/I get that CEO role/I land that big account. In the 'I'll be satisfied when...' process, we aren't satisfied with our current situation. We do not get the small dopamine hits along the way. Worse, we risk cortisol overload because our brain feels like we are under threat until we accomplish that big goal. Then when we achieve that goal, the dopamine is great but short-lived, and we hunt for something bigger. This process is unhealthy and unsustainable.

———

Why know the messengers?

Our animal brain is wanting to protect us. If we can understand this with our executive brain, we have greater ability to recognise our response to 'threat' and consciously seek out the things that will release the good chemicals in the brain. If we do not, our pattern-seeking brain will start to see very unhelpful patterns. Patterns that convince us we are under threat. Patterns that keep triggering negative thoughts and further cortisol that affect our mental health. We then go sliding down that continuum.

Our animal brain is seeking safety through a sense of belonging and predictability. That we are part of a tribe that values what we bring. That the tribe will look after us if we are vulnerable. That the tribe will help us make sense of the world—creating a pattern for us. In understanding the role these messengers play, we have a greater ability to consciously create the circumstances in which they will be triggered in the right doses. If you maintain optimal mental health, you will still slip down to yellow. You are only human. But you can bring yourself back faster if you get to know these messengers well.

Think about things inside and outside of work that can trigger these messengers. People often think about oxytocin in a home setting. I am part of a large family—one of nine—and we all think a bit differently, but nothing is better than a family gathering with my brothers and sisters and mum. There is an absolute sense of belonging together in the laughter that we share as a family, and that makes us feel good. My family is my primary tribe. My brain registers this as a safe environment. So, I will hunt that out myself to get oxytocin when I feel I need it.

Brilliant teamwork can have the same effect of triggering oxytocin with the added benefit of serotonin and dopamine when you set out to achieve a task and then deliver on it because of combined strength. What have you done recently with a group of people where you have left with an absolute buzz of being with people who 'get you'? That is the oxytocin talking. What goals have you recently achieved that left you pumping the air? That is the dopamine talking. What recognition have you been given recently by others that made you feel great? That is the serotonin talking. It can be hard for some people to believe that they are not entirely in control. We are so conscious of our executive brain. This brain that can think about complex issues and drive us to make changes to deliver for our organisation. I see this resistance in coaching at times. This belief that we can be wholly rational and are always consciously choosing what we do. But the science says otherwise. This animal brain of ours really does have a mind of its own. It wants us to survive. If we do not make wise choices that helps keep this internal balance, it will 'fight' to bring us back to balance. Have constant colds or get the flu? Our body

PRACTICAL STEPS:

Understanding the effect of key chemicals on how you feel

Make a table with four columns and write oxytocin (connection/ belonging), serotonin (recognition/value), dopamine (achievement/reward) and cortisol (stress/challenges) as the column headings. Go back to the reflections on days you felt you were in green versus yellow (from the previous practical steps box in this chapter). In those days you are feeling in the green, what events took place that made you feel particularly good. What messenger do you think it triggered? (could be more than one). Write that event down. Then on days in the yellow, again what event/s may have triggered cortisol? If you just spend a little bit of time each week starting to raise your awareness of how your body is reacting to things, it will help you in future chapters to build up the muscle of influence over those chemicals.

TABLE ONE Learning to listen to the chemicals in the brain

	OXYTOCIN Connection & belonging	SEROTONIN Recognised & valued	DOPAMINE Achievement & predictions come true	CORTISOL Stress/ challenges
MONDAY				
TUESDAY				
WEDNESDAY				
THURSDAY				
FRIDAY				
SATURDAY				
SUNDAY				
Q: WHAT HAS TRIGGERED THE MESSENGERS TODAY?				

is overworked. We have not taken enough steps to look after it. It is the warning signal to do something different. The stomach upset. The lack of sleep. The tension in our muscles. Significant signs to make changes—to find your way back to a better balanced internal eco-system. The same happens with our mental health.

It is only the sociopaths or psychopaths in the world that do not feel emotions the way the majority of us do. For the rest of us, there are always these underlying emotions that are being triggered by these messengers. We need to understand what they are trying to do for us if we want to influence them to perform.

Still trying to convince yourself it is not you?

Many managers feel they do not want to admit their vulnerabilities. They do not want to acknowledge when their heart pounds; when they cannot sleep; when they cannot stop their over-thinking executive brain; when they feel like they are a fraud.

Picture 150 people in a conference room. A few years ago, I found myself in a McKinsey course in a conference room full of executives across big Australian organisations. We had only known each other for a few days then. A lecture from Susan David[*] took us through an exercise to reflect on who we were and for what we stood. At one point, we had to open our workbook and complete an activity. The page read, 'I am...', and there was a yellow sticky note stuck to the page. Susan told

------

[*] Susan David, PhD, is a psychologist on the faculty of Harvard Medical School, cofounder and codirector of the Institute of Coaching at McLean Hospital and CEO of Evidence Based Psychology.

us to complete that sentence with our deepest, darkest fear about ourselves.

We had already been talking about journaling and how sometimes writing down our thoughts on a piece of paper, then screwing the paper up and throwing it away can be a powerful way of not letting a story take over. Most of us were assuming, therefore, that we were writing this as part of reflection, then screwing it up and throwing it in the bin. We finished the exercise and continued with the lecture. After about 15 minutes, she said, 'I want you to go back to that exercise with the sticky note and stick it on your chest.'

The level of tension in the room increased significantly. The looks of discomfort, if not terror on faces around the room were evident. I do not know about everyone else, but my heart was racing at a million miles an hour. Then she said, 'I want you to stand up, imagine yourself at a cocktail party and introduce yourself to as many people as you can in this short time. The rule, however, is you must introduce yourself not by your name but by your deepest, darkest fear.'

You could sense the level of sheer panic in this room. But once the conversation started, what was apparent was a common theme. Everyone has deep dark fears. They may not want to admit them or even fully understand them. But they are there. By far, the majority of concerns in this room were based around being inadequate or a fraud. This acknowledgement, however, would have never come out in general conversation in a group of senior managers.

We are all vulnerable. It is a complex world we face. One in which we do not even know all the problems we will encounter, let alone their solutions. We have had our first significant challenge working out what to do during a pandemic. Our animal brains are working overtime, trying to find patterns in complexity and where the threats are. We are all vulnerable on that continuum. The COVID-19 pandemic has, I believe, helped everyone understand how vulnerable we all are, bringing to the surface feelings that may have hidden previously. You might not yet want to acknowledge it to other people, but the vulnerability is there.

It is important to breathe through this discomfort because there are simple things that you can do to continue to build the strength of your mental health for what lies ahead.

———

Maslow got it wrong?

Remember Maslow's hierarchy of needs[*]? For a refresher, see Figure Four. Maslow identified that the first hierarchy of needs[*] for humans was entirely physical—food, water etc. It was only as a person satisfied their needs from one layer of the hierarchy that they could move up to the next. Right in the middle of the five tiers is social belonging (or love). We have accepted this ranking as being correct for decades. It is only in more recent years that people have started to question the assumptions of this hierarchy.

What we see now is that connection is just as important, believe it or not, as food and water to our basic survival (see Figure Five). Remember those wild animals outside the cave? We are fundamentally hardwired to connect with other people. Our brains need to feel that connection to send the signal to our body it is safe. Without the feeling of safety that connection brings, the mind can go into overload searching for threats. How we connect helps us to get through challenges. If we are isolated, our chemicals override us, we do not perform, and we do not cope.

---

[*] A.H. Maslow (1943) originally published in Psychological Review, 50, 370–396.

FIGURE FOUR

Maslow's hierarchy on human health and potential

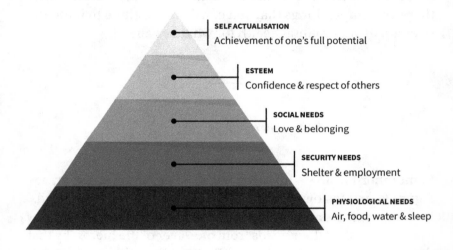

In the 1960s, Harry Harlow controversially undertook a range of experiments on Rhesus monkeys, starving them of social interaction[*]. After taking them out of isolation, they exhibited significant anti-social and autistic behaviour. If not isolated for too long, social contact could curb these behaviours eventually, but there was a failure to thrive. While these investigations were considered controversial, it has shaped recommendations on the importance of social connection to babies and young children's thriving and spawned significant further research.

---

[*] Harlow, H.F., Dobsworth, R.O. and Harlow, M.K. (1965) Total Social Isolation in Monkeys, Department of Psychology, Primate Laboratory and Regional Primate Research Centre, University of Wisconsin. Read before the Academy, April 28, 1965.

FIGURE FIVE
Rethinking Maslow's hierarchy on human health and potential

SELF ACTUALISATION
Achievement of one's full potential

SECURITY
Shelter & employment

ESTEEM
Confidence & respect of others

PHYSIOLOGICAL
Air, food, water & sleep

SOCIAL CONNECTION
Love & belonging

This study is now influencing our understanding of connection for adults.

We have to appreciate that we all need connection. We all need to feel we belong. You may think that family is enough—that is your safe environment. However, if you do not experience this safety at work, you are not going to be able to perform at your best.

In a world where technology connects us across the globe, we have never been more disconnected from people. That sense of loneliness is increasing and raising alarm bells for governments around the world. Two meta-analyses (reviews of results from a large number of studies) conducted by Holt-Lusted, a professor of psychology and colleagues, identified that loneliness and social isolation might increase risk of premature death by up to 50 per cent*. Dr Vivek H. Murty, a former Surgeon General of the United States, wrote an article for the Harvard Business Review reporting loneliness and weak social connections have a similar effect to smoking 15 cigarettes a day.†

Robert Waldinger, is the fourth Director of the Harvard Study of Adult Development that was conducted over 75 years, and multiple generations. The research identified that the most significant indicator of health and wellbeing in old age is quality of relationships. Not socioeconomic background, not opportunities, not genes. But rather good relationships—connection. This connection is more important than anything else. If you can build that sense of belonging, your animal brain feels less threatened. It creates a buffer for us, from the inevitable challenges of life. This sense of safety from connection enables you to perform now and be able to enjoy life for longer.

It is useful, when you think about this concept of connection, to reflect on a recent challenge that you have had. It might have been missing a deadline, not achieving a high performance review, not meeting a target or working hard to deliver and not being recognised. Think of what happened subsequently. Did you not sleep? Could you not stop thinking about it? Did you feel angry, frustrated or annoyed and took it out on someone else. That is what it feels like with cortisol running through your body. Your animal brain sees these events as threats, whether or not your executive brain is fully aware of it. Threat leads to cortisol, designed to put you on alert. Not counteracting this means a slide down the continuum for a short or an extended period.

---

*   Whiteman, H. (2017) Loneliness a bigger killer than obesity says researchers. Medical News Today, August 6, 2017.

†   Loneliness is a serious public health problem. The Economist. September 1, 2018.

What is the 'Mental Health Pie'?

In needing to find the balance in our internal eco-system, no one person or activity will consistently be the person or thing you connect with to solve all your problems. You need to have a balance of different actions you can take to get the right balance in these messengers to optimise your mental health, much like changing a recipe to suit your needs. One ingredient doesn't make a recipe. It is the combination where the magic is created.

I like to describe what you need to do to look after your mental health in terms of the *Mental Health Pie*. This outlook is perhaps influenced by a trip to London, where I saw the Broadway show, *Waitress*. I love the analogy of the changing pie used throughout the show.

There are essential ingredients that always need to be in this pie to make it work, but the quantity of these ingredients and how they are combined can vary—to suit what you need on that particular day.

There are four core ingredients to look after your mental health:
- Connecting to self,
- Connecting to others,
- Contribution,
- Curiosity.

The components of this pie are not plucked from the sky. Research continues to support that these ingredients are critical,[*] albeit different language may be used.

---

[*] www.beyondblue.org.au – Beyond Blue booklets: A guide to what works for depression and A guide to what works for anxiety.

The Mental Health Pie

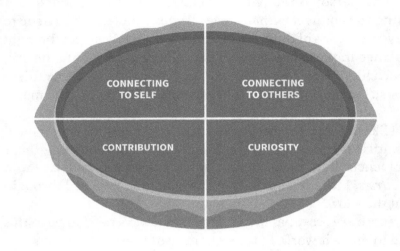

Connecting to self

Greater awareness of and respect for our own physical body, thoughts and emotions enables us to make better decisions for the short and long term that build mental health. Our physical and mental health are intertwined. How you eat, exercise and sleep will significantly influence your mental state. How you learn to control the classroom inside your head with its swirling emotions and thoughts also impacts your mental health. Connection to self is the heightened awareness that enables you to identify when your different messenger chemicals are triggered. Which, in turn, allows you to influence your body and mind to look after both your physical and mental health.

Connecting to others

Given that we are hard-wired for connection for survival, which triggers the wonderful oxytocin, it would be no surprise to you that connection to others is a framework ingredient. We are social creatures and quality—not quantity—of real connection and genuinely being seen by others, is incredibly powerful to keep our brains feeling safe and not triggering too much cortisol.

Contribution

Contribution can present at different levels depending on what you define as your tribe. It can be the higher-level concept of leaving a legacy by what we do for an organisation, community or society down to each day choosing to help someone at work or home because of your skills. You need to think about contribution in the context of getting a 'hit' of serotonin. We feel better when we are helping others because our brain is recognising a strength that we have that makes us valuable in our tribe. Our sense of value to our tribe (no matter how big or small) keeps the right balance of serotonin.

Curiosity

Remember our pattern-seeking brain which loves rewards? Learning new things, i.e. working out a pattern, is food for the brain. Finding this 'brain food' does not mean embarking on a PhD or even a formal learning course—although completing such things triggers a large amount of both serotonin and dopamine! It can be as small as being curious when something goes wrong at work, rather than becoming frustrated or angry, which can trigger cortisol. Curiosity, this desire to learn, helps us seek out a cause and effect and act. It helps us create a new pattern. Curiosity can also be fed by hobbies, reading about historical events, doing crosswords or exploring a new place on holidays. Curiosity helps us detach from the vicious cycle of negative emotions, enabling our brains to switch into a different mode.

We will be talking about these ingredients in more detail in Chapter Five. I will show you how to understand what will work for you to build up a connection to self, connection to others, your contribution and your curiosity. For the moment, it's knowing there is a rational scientific reason for why we feel the way we do. The more you understand what is going on with those chemicals and the related thought processes, the better ability you will have to keep in green longer. Likewise, you will quickly recognise when you have shifted to yellow and pull yourself back before you slide into orange. Ultimately that is the aim of the book.

———

What choices are you making?

With physical health, we understand that it is a combination of nutrition, sleeping and exercise that is important. You may not always be great at it. Still, the more responsibility you take on at leadership levels, the more you appreciate how important your physical health is, to being able to deliver sustainably. You have to start thinking about your mental health the same way you think about your physical health. You have to make choices every day that builds up this health which enables sustainable delivery.

Perhaps the *Mental Health Pie* is not the healthiest analogy given pie could be fattening—although I have been known to eat an occasional doughnut for my mental health! But this *Mental Health Pie* is scientifically based. Sometimes it takes a severe physical illness, possibly life-threatening, for people to 'wake up' and recognise that their daily choices need to be changed. But this change is a long road back to health. You need to think about your mental health in the same way. If you wait until you are in the orange or red to create that right combination of connection to self and others with contribution and curiosity, it is so much harder to get back to green. When cortisol floods your brain, it needs the patterns you have previously built up to recognise it is safe. No one is immune. You can, and will, slide down that scale. The good thing is that there are practical things you can do to get back to green.

Just like with your physical health, you can get this pie working for you and stay in the healthier green and occasional yellow range. But it takes ongoing commitment, just like it does with exercise, sleep and diet. I would like to think that, being an expert in this space, I had it all under control. But several years ago, I was in a particularly difficult space. I ended up so exhausted with everything that was going on that I just needed some time out. I went to see my GP, who had known me for a long time, and he gave me some advice:

'Every day, you need to spend 20 minutes doing something that is just for you. Every week, you need to spend an hour doing something that is just for you. And every month you need to spend a day doing something just for you. And by the way, that does not mean reading stories to the kids. And knowing you, you need to diarise these times otherwise they will not happen.'

It reflected how bad a state I was in at that time, that when I came home, I got stressed out about my stress management because I did not know what to do in that 'me' time. It was a great realisation of how much I had focused on my external world of running a business, completing my MBA and raising young kids. As I write this, I feel tired. No wonder I was burning out! I was so

Investment in you, a day, a week, a month

While you work through this book, I suggest you kick-start thinking about your day, your week, your month. This connection to self-awareness is the first of the base ingredients. What are you doing for *your* 20 minutes per day, an hour per week, a day per month that renews your energy for the big picture?

focused on longer-term external goals that I was not putting my oxygen mask on first. It was almost as if I thought I was invincible. But negative changes were slowly creeping up on me.

It took me a while to ground myself back through the four ingredients of the *Mental Health Pie*. It was a wake-up call for me to recognise I had fallen into the trap of yellow being the new green and was slowly slipping into the orange. Because of the levels of cortisol, it then took an extended effort to build new patterns. Patterns in which I did not feel guilty for doing activities that got the oxytocin and serotonin going, while my do-to list was a mile long.

I would say that the way people publicise or teach mental health does not always resonate with me. Because the things that bring me a real sense of connection, contribution and curiosity are different to the next person because of our own background experiences. I am not going to give you a prescription of precisely what you should do to connect, contribute or spark curiosity. The same as there is never one way to improve your physical health. It is your choice, and you have to find out what works for you. The critical point to remember is that connection contribution and curiosity build our mental health.

Key things to remember

- ALL of us move up and down the continuum of mental health, just as we can with physical health.
- You have an animal brain that is always working to keep you alive. It continually looks for threats—physical and psychological—that means it's unsafe and patterns that indicate safety—or not.
- There are chemicals in your animal brain responding to threats and safety which trigger you to move around on the continuum instead of staying in green.
- If you are threatened—physically or psychologically—your brain releases cortisol.
- If you feel like you belong in your 'tribe', your brain releases oxytocin making you feel safe.
- If you feel valued for the contribution you make, your brain releases serotonin making you feel safe.
- If you achieve goals you set out to achieve, your brain releases dopamine which makes you feel good.
- Connection is as vital as air, food and water.
- Connection to self and others, curiosity and contribution, are ways of training the animal brain to release those chemicals in the right balance to enable you to perform at your best.

It does not mean that you will not get wobbly sometimes. But if you have got those factors in place, you reduce the likelihood of deep slides down the continuum. And when you do get wobbly and land yourself in yellow, it enables you to pull it back before you slide to orange.

In Brené Brown's book *Rising Strong**, she includes a quote from Asaro tribe of Indonesia and Papua New Guinea: "Knowledge is

---

* Brown, Brené. (2015) Rising Strong. Penguin Random House UK.

only a rumour until it lives in the muscle." You might know, you might get it, but you need to make it a habit. That is where the challenge kicks in. In Chapter Nine we will explore how to make it 'sticky', but in the meantime, I would recommend that you introduce the continuum concept and the day, week and month concept to at least one or two people that you completely trust have got your back. Then start using this language to check in with each other. How often you are going into yellow and what is bringing you back through the choices you are making to put your oxygen mask on each day, each week, each month?

Now that you understand the context of what is happening inside the brain, let's delve into how your mind and the influence of others can create a shadow—unspoken but felt. As a leader, you need to connect to self and understand this shadow to build the connection that leads to high performance.

CHAPTER THREE

THE CLASSROOM AND THE SHADOW

Have you ever walked out of a meeting where a colleague comments to you about how intense, rude or critical someone else was? Do you then wonder whether you were actually at the same meeting as you thought it was fine? Or have you had a one to one conversation with someone, and they suddenly get angry, upset or withdrawn, and you do not quite understand why? Or you later hear via someone else that they reacted negatively to your conversation despite appearing fine during the discussion? As far as you were concerned, there was nothing much in your exchange. Yet they are critical of YOUR behaviour.

There is much energy wasted in organisations due to misinterpretations, misunderstandings and people's inability to communicate effectively with each other.

Why? Because of the classrooms inside our collective heads that we talked about in chapter two. These collective classrooms cast unnecessary 'shadows', creating disconnection, that impact on mental health and performance.

In this chapter, we will explore what happens when two brains process a situation in entirely different ways. In the context of being a leader, step one is accepting that you need to look after your mental health. The next step is recognising that you can inadvertently impact other people's mental health and contribute to them sliding into yellow. You are casting your 'shadow'. Not intentionally, but for two reasons.

Firstly, the inconsistency of *your* words—*your* conscious intention—with the classroom inside your head—the emotions and internal monologue.

Secondly, how *their* brain interprets your actions and words— the classroom inside *their* head.

Before you say, 'But that is their problem', remember, you will not deliver sustainably on your own. It is a team effort. And a team of brains flooded with cortisol is not what is going to provide the best effort. If your team see a constant threat, they will have a continuous cortisol release. Your role as a leader is to trigger healthy levels of oxytocin, serotonin and dopamine in your teams. That is what helps deliver peak performance. You are not responsible for their mental health. They have to own their mental health like they need to own their physical health. But you can help their mental health and therefore performance by owning your own shadow.

Your understanding of the shape of your shadow and how it changes gives you the power to connect in a much healthier way that leads to better performance AND better health for all involved.

One of the best 'ah-ha' moments for me as a leader was understanding the idea that we judge ourselves by our intent and others by their behaviour*. We ALL do this unconsciously. We believe that because our intention is right, if the other person reacts poorly, then it is their issue, not ours. If we want to get the best from our team, we need to understand what is going on inside that person's head impacts how they interpret everything. We also have to realise that sometimes because of our classroom inside our head, what we say and our body language completely mismatch. We kid ourselves that we are better actors than we are. We think we have our anger, frustration, annoyance or worry hidden. We choose the right words, but body language causes an unwanted shadow and it is your problem. The person observes your body language and words, not your unspoken intention, and interprets this based on the impact on them. Your intention is irrelevant. It is how they feel impacted that matters to them. Even though it can be frustrating how people misinterpret, if you want the best results, you need to understand that it is common for your intent not to meet its intended mark.

In my role, assisting in resolving conflict, I observe time and again that it is the shadow (the unspoken but felt), that invariably causes the problem. One person claims the other person behaved in an aggressive inappropriate or threatening way; the other person becomes defensive. Their recollection of the situation is entirely different. They each defend their view that they are right, and the other person is wrong. If there are witnesses to an event, it is useful to confirm the actual words or body movements that took place (depending on the reliability of the witness' memory). However the witness does not know how those involved are processing the words they are hearing. They do not understand what is happening with the classroom inside each person's head.

---

* Covey, S.R. (1990). The Seven Habits of Highly Effective People. Simon & Schuster Inc. New York. New York.

At the time, the shadow is hidden. It only becomes apparent when one person explains the impact of the conversation. But if not explained well, the other person becomes defensive. And on goes the vicious cycle.

In Chapter Two, I called out the power of connection. You cannot underestimate how powerful it is when a team can communicate effectively through inevitable conflict that occurs in any environment.

> *Your organisation or department performance will exceed all expectations if you can harness the insights you gain from having great conversations about where disconnection has occurred.*

But it is hard. So many people do not have the skills to have effective conversations. In this chapter, I want to help you understand why everyone casts unintentional shadows, how you can learn more about your shadow and how you can identify when your classroom inside your head sees shadows that are not there. Shadows can be unintentionally positive, but it is the negative shadow that is the challenge. The negative shadow is our pattern-seeking brains seeing threat and triggering cortisol. Often illogically. And we know where that ends up. So, you need to learn the way of the shadow.

Why should I be concerned about my shadow?

If you are getting focused on being 'right' because you know what your intended impact is, you are ultimately destroying connection. In turn, affecting relationships and ultimately, performance. Remember John Lennon's quote "life is what happens when you are busy making other plans"? Well, disconnection is what can happen when you are busy making other plans. This shadow can wreak havoc.

People who have not had enough opportunities to reflect on good specific feedback tend to underestimate or disregard their shadow. They are convinced they know themselves well and what they are intentionally doing in their conversations. They tend to believe that if the other person reacts negatively, it is that person's problem, not theirs. It is true that how the other person reacts does say far more about what is happening at that moment for the other person. And that person needs to own and deal with their responses. But come back to your role as a leader. As a leader, you need to influence others, so they want to follow you. So, they want to work with you to deliver your objectives. If you disregard the classroom inside the other person's head, then you will not get the best from them. You are not responsible for the classroom inside their head—they are. They have to learn how to control it consciously. But if you do not accept that you cast a shadow, you will keep causing unnecessary disconnection, which decreases performance. Understanding points of potential disconnection enables you to minimise them.

Even if you currently have teams which all seem to be working well together, which can be rare as hens' teeth, you will keep working with different people all the time. Each time you are working with different people, that intent versus impact shifts.

You have got to be attuned to that, to make sure that your shadow does not trigger disconnection through cortisol.

Intent versus impact can operate in your personal life as much as in your business life. I am not about to go into your relationships outside of work and how to work on these. But I want you to understand that when you find yourself in any conversation outside of work and you are asking yourself, 'How on earth did I end up in this space?' it is invariably that same answer. The 'shadow' has caused this disconnection because what you think you are saying with intent is not reading the same way with the other person.

Neurologist Robert Burton* explains how our brain likes predictable storytelling. We look for patterns because it gives us some sense of certainty. That is dopamine at work. Our brain loves to predict and see a pattern play out. Once we have a belief in our minds, the animal brain encourages us to interpret what we see with that particular view in mind.

Ever bought a new car and in the weeks leading up to getting it from the dealer, you suddenly notice that same type of car far more on the road? Hello, dopamine! This response is your brain looking for a pattern. If you believe someone is 'in your corner', you will interpret all their behaviours that way. The brain looks for a pattern that reinforces the 'rule' or belief. It is a cognitive bias we have. Likewise, if you believe someone is not supportive of you, it is easy to interpret their behaviours negatively. Brené Brown† reminds us to "stop walking through the world looking for confirmation that you do not belong". If you are looking for signs of not belonging, you will always find it because your brain is seeking that pattern.

Our interpretation of a pattern of behaviour can also be a pattern of absent behaviour. With one manager, I felt that they

---

* Robert A. Burton MD is a neurologist and graduate of Yale University and the University of California who has written numerous books on the neurosciences including 'On being certain: Believing you are right even when you are not'.
† Brown, Brené. (2015) Rising Strong. Penguin Random House UK

had absolute confidence in me to deliver. I would not talk to them often. I interpreted that absence of communication as confidence in what I was doing.

Then I worked with a manager that I believed *did not* have confidence in me. There was a length of time without talking to them, and my cortisol kicked in. I interpreted the silence as them not caring about me and what I was delivering—that I was not that important to them and their goals. When I was thinking like that, I was not performing at my best. The irony of this is it can be a self-fulfilling prophecy—luckily not in my case. If someone reporting to you for whatever reason believes you do not have confidence in them, the vicious cortisol cycle begins. They start to perform below their best because of their belief and the impact of this initial cortisol release. You then see poor performance which triggers further cortisol within them. If only you could have caught that shadow earlier!

I was interpreting the same behaviour from both of my managers in two different ways. Indeed, their lack of interaction, in both cases, had nothing to do with my performance and everything to do with what was going on for them. But try convincing my pattern-seeking brain at that point in time! I received a benefit from the positive interpretation but needed a 'circuit breaker' to get myself refocused after the contrary analysis.

The shadow exists because our brains are continually scanning for threats. The past experiences of each person and the range of current issues influence the perceived threat of the situation. When all is good outside work, and there is a *minor* work performance blip, the brain will still detect this as a threat, but the pattern-seeking brain can recognise this as a minor threat. When things are tough both outside, and inside work, when relationships are not healthy, and there is a small blip, the brain can go into panic mode. Despite all your good intentions, the individual will interpret everything you say with a heightened concern about their job security, their bonus or their relationship with you.

The shadow can also exist because your words do not always match your body language. You can intentionally choose your words very carefully. You can even have someone else help script them for you. But the emotions that are raging inside you cannot help but show. You are just not that good at acting, or you think you are so good at acting that you bury every emotion, keeping them controlled. But the lack of emotion in your conversation casts the shadow. The other person cannot work out how to connect because they do not see you showing any emotion that might indicate you care.

When both parties feel under duress the most significant shadow forms. As a manager, you are saying the right things but not believing the words and you will be quick to interpret their response negatively. The other person, due to their threat response is interpreting everything you say and do with a negative lens as well, causing significant disconnection. This disconnect is why you must be concerned about your shadow.

Is the shadow always bad?

The interesting flip on the shadow is that it can have a positive impact on someone without this being your intention. Drew Dudley's TED Talk on Everyday Leadership explains a simple but powerful example of the positive effects of casting a shadow. In this scenario, Drew had an intent of generating laughter and awareness of university services in a group of people waiting to enrol at the University. For one person in that line, Drew's action flipped her from a cortisol overload due to her anxiety, to a rush of oxytocin, from a sense of belonging that the laughter generated. That laughter in turn introduced her to the person standing beside her in line who became her future partner. It is a brilliant example of an unintended but powerful positive shadow.

I remember a team member of mine, giving me feedback on the level of confidence I had built in them in the way I responded in a particular meeting. I had told the rest of the team 'this person has got this!'. My intent at the time was not specifically to build confidence. It was to communicate directly in the group who would deliver and refocus the rest of the team. I also did not see the need to intervene to enable them to perform—I knew they could. This exchange was, however, an example of a positive shadow. For what was going on in the other person's mind, my comment had a far more significant positive impact than my direct intent. I only knew this because they took the time to give me feedback.

How can I better understand my shadow?

Feedback is the key. There is no expectation of understanding every small impact you have on the team. There is no expectation of understanding everyone's classroom inside their head that creates these shadows. Truth be told you will not always be able to ultimately work out why *your* brain has processed some things in a particular way. Understanding your shadow is not about your team explaining everything going on inside their heads. It is about them being able to say, 'When we had that interaction, you said this and I walked away feeling angry or frustrated, and I am pretty sure that is not your intent, so could you help me understand what your intent was?'—THIS is the way you truly get to understand your shadow. Your team taking the time and being prepared to explain your impact. Then for you to reflect on your intent to work out how much was your classroom mismatching your words and body language versus how much was it the other person's classroom. When someone else is prepared to give you this feedback, you can learn not only about your impact, but help reduce cortisol release for the other person.

Watching what people are saying and doing after an interaction with you enables you to understand and control your shadow more effectively. Remember if someone thinks they do not belong, the pattern-seeking brain cannot help but look for behaviours that reinforce this. If you observe a response from someone that seems at odds with what you wanted the impact to be, there is a classroom inside that other person's head that has created a shadow. You need to ask more questions so you can provide the clarity, recognition or connection they need to reduce the cortisol. The reduction in cortisol shrinks that shadow. In turn, you learn more about their classroom and can make a conscious choice to alter your behaviour to bring your impact closer to your intent. If you want to get the best from your team, you have got to be able to get your team understanding intent and impact do not always match. That we all unintentionally create a negative shadow.

Sometimes, the more senior you are, the harder it is to get honest and specific feedback about your shadow. Your colleagues or team may not be confident or competent to give the feedback that you need. Where you can come unstuck though is when you stick with, 'Give me some feedback. Tell me how I am going.' It is too broad. A way to learn more about your unintentional shadow is to plan for 'forward feedback' from others. *Before* a meeting, talk to a couple of team members about what your intention is for the session (inspire the team; get everyone energised; provide clarity on direction or current performance; get them focused on delivery for the next month etc.). Whatever your intention might be, ask them to give you specific examples after the meeting that had the intended impact or had a different impression. You want to keep learning whether your intent landed with the effect that you wanted. Specific situational feedback like this can start to give you some useful insights. This method is less threatening to the team and valuable to you. Helping you understand your shadow and the classroom inside the collective heads of the group. When you get feedback that intent and impact match, you get a great dopamine rush. Being open to this feedback also builds trust with the team. Trust makes the team feel safe, and in turn, safety lowers the cortisol. What a great combination for peak performance! You better understand your shadow and create a mentally healthy environment for the team.

_____

What is happening with the 'classroom inside my head' that is impacting me?

No matter how good you think you are or how confident you are, you are human. Also, you are in a high-pressured job with challenges that will arise. For everyone, at times, some things going on inside our head create a greater sense of negativity. A darker shadow than we would like. For you, it could be that a target was not hit, or the support you thought you had from your colleagues for a particular position fell away at a critical moment. Maybe you fought with your partner, child or parent that morning, or even you are late for work because of bad traffic. This list could go on. Life happens and it impacts our ability to be fully present in the conversation, ensuring intent versus impact match on any particular day. Without always realising it, your mind's classroom focusses on things that are not right rather than all the things that are. Those life events are 'threats'. They trigger increased cortisol. A small amount of cortisol creates focus, allowing you to act to get into a better headspace. But when cortisol keeps coming, and you ignore it, this classroom inside your head will cast a shadow.

If you can recognise your impact because of your classroom, you can repair the disconnection this has caused. If you can identify when you have not landed an interaction in the right way, you can address it. A leader takes accountability for their impact. Others will respect you more for owning your impact. If you do not, your team are left wondering, and their brains trigger chemicals and thought processes in an unhelpful way. As Brené Brown says[*],

"Even if we have the insight to know that our boss... blew up at us because something tender was triggered, and it's not actually about us, it still shatters trust and respect... working... on eggshells creates huge cracks in our sense of safety and self-worth."

Whenever you find yourself reacting negatively to a conversation, it is always worth asking yourself what the classroom inside your head is talking about right now. What else is going on that makes you feel more 'threatened' by this conversation?

Remember those interactions you noted down in chapter two that you were classifying as triggering cortisol? Those experiences that left you with those mild feelings of being annoyed, irritated or frustrated? It is not useful on an ongoing basis to dissect and analyse every conversation. However, when you are first

---

[*] Brown, Brené. (2015) Rising Strong. Penguin Random House UK.

learning to understand the classroom inside your head, this is a helpful place to start. For each of the situations that you believe triggered cortisol, you need to figure out what was going on in the classroom inside your head. How is your brain processing what is happening as a threat to you? Likely, you do not consciously think that the incident or event is actually a threat. But a negative emotion is indicating that your animal brain is feeling overloaded in some way. As Susan David says[*] "Emotion is data, not direction". In other words;

Your reaction is telling you your animal brain does not like what is happening. It is up to you to work out why then choose what to do.

- Of what internal talk in your 'classroom' were you aware?
- What assumptions were you making about the other person?
- If you start from the assumption that the other person was not deliberately aiming to annoy, irritate or frustrate, then what do you think their intent was?
- What was happening for you on that day that meant you could not see their intent as clearly? Were you tired or distracted by other things? Had something else already gone wrong?

Any time you are feeling frustrated about an interaction, stop and ask yourself, 'What is going on inside my head that is influencing how I am interpreting this situation? How can I get myself into a better space to understand their intent versus how it's landed for me?' When we seriously reflect, we can find that it is other pressures that cause us not to see that particular interaction positively. It is not anything to do with them. It is our classroom that is interfering in the conversation and causing the shadow.

---

[*] David, Susan. PhD. (2016). Emotional Agility: Get Unstuck, Embrace Change, and Thrive in Work and Life. Penguin. Random House. New York.

We will all slip into yellow. It is normal. You just want to work to avoid sliding into the orange. Negative emotions that are more than fleeting are a good indicator that you have a bit too much cortisol in your body, and your classroom inside your head is not helping you. Recognise these emotions. Get curious about what has triggered them and how you can then change them. This builds your mental health.

How can connection shrink the negative shadow talk?

I can remember having a conversation with my manager when I was new in a role about what a Board Paper should contain. I left the meeting feeling somewhat uncomfortable about what I believed the suggestion to be. Hello, shadow! I had a choice at that point. I could write what I thought he wanted and feel uncomfortable, or I could talk with him again. I chose the latter. It was uncomfortable to raise the point with him, to acknowledge that it didn't sit right with me, and to seek clarification of his intent versus the impact on me. It was also a huge relief. He was able to explain his intent, which sat far better with me—enabling me to write a Board Paper that pleased both of us. But far more important than this, it built a connection. It meant that we both became increasingly comfortable with raising issues with each other—in turn enabling a focus for both of us on high performance.

Connection shrinks the shadow, through a two-way process between people. It is where both people feel they are understood and accepted by the other. It does not happen overnight. It does not mean there are no disagreements, nor imply a lack of conflict.

What it means is that both parties are comfortable in:
- Owning that they have a shadow
- Being open to feedback on their shadow
- Giving feedback on the other person's shadow

It is where there is high trust. There is comfort to express views, debate views, argue opinions. Comfortable that you have each other's backs. Where shadows appear, then quickly disappear. Connection shrinks the unnecessary shadow that distracts and interferes with performance.

As managers move their way up in an organisation, they often become more confident in saying, 'This is the way I do things, the way I have always done things and this is what I think needs to happen.' But ultimately, if you do not remember that you create shadows, you risk becoming too confident in the way you 'communicate' and will not get the connection and therefore performance you need from the team.

How often have you had feedback when someone says, 'You never told us about that'? Yet you know yourself you have 'communicated'? This is a classic 'classroom inside the head moment'. Even when you have evidence of the actual 'communication', what the other person heard is influenced by what is happening for them.

If you understand how to shrink your negative shadow, you can trigger oxytocin, which creates a sense of connection and trust that leads to performance.

If you do not build a two-way connection, you will not be able to understand when your intent and impact do not match—you miss out on high performance. Those you interact with can be confused, uncertain, not valued, not understood, and you have no idea. Your communication is triggering cortisol without you realising, and you will not get the performance that you want in the team.

Minimising the negative shadow

If you have not had many conversations with your team on connection, they may not understand. But connection is how you minimise the shadow. My recommendation to start building one to one connection is three-fold:

Have conversations informally (at the coffee machine), or formally (team meetings) where you work to understand what each of your team does outside work. Work out from that, what is the common link between you. It could be the type of coffee; that you have kids, that you share a love (or hate) of cats etc. Some form of common ground is the first step to belonging in 'the tribe' that you lead.

Focus on how you can trigger dopamine and serotonin by setting clear goals and celebrating their contribution to the achievement of these. As the animal brain sees more evidence that our skills are valued, we are more likely to trust that person. Trust decreases the shadow.

If you have said something and you can see by the facial reaction or the comments that they are feeling defensive, pause and ask them, 'My intention is this, but I sense from how you are reacting here that that is not the case for you. Tell me what is going on for you.' These simple actions—understanding what connection means, building connection through recognition and calling it when you think disconnection has occurred, unlock performance.

Expand this to the exercise mentioned earlier in the chapter. Tell one or two team members before a meeting the impact you want, asking them to note what you did that did or did not have an effect. Be open afterwards to the feedback. Thank them for it. Seek to modify something in the next meeting because of it; this builds trust, which creates connection.

Key things to remember

- Your intent and your impact will not always match. Nor will your manager's, or your team's.
- This is because there is a 'classroom' inside your head and the other person's head.
- This classroom is driven by how our brain processes the world and what chemicals get triggered because of this.
- When one or both parties have increased cortisol in their brain and do not have a strong relationship with this other person, these 'classrooms' can create a negative shadow—not spoken but felt.
- The negative shadow creates disconnection if it is not diminished.
- Connection (the opposite of disconnection) is at the heart of mental health AND excellent performance.
- If you can build awareness of the shadow, then you can influence how big or small it is and strengthen connection.
- As a leader, you have to own your shadow and your classroom if you want to have the best chance at consistent high performance.

The most important thing is to recognise when you suspect intent does not match impact. When you can understand that a shadow has appeared, you can call it, enabling you to reconnect with the other person. You have that ability to pause the cortisol and get the oxytocin of connection back—to get the best performance from people.

We are all human, we have all got baggage, and we have all got these classrooms that do all sorts of funny things. It is not about being perfect or going into therapy for everything that you need to do. It is about understanding that, regardless of what you intend to do, there is a shadow that you cast. You have got to be able to understand that shadow and how to shrink the negative shadow if you want to get the best results. As Brené Brown says[*], "Using our ability to navigate uncomfortable conversations, own our emotions and rumble with our stories is how we build connection."

I hope that you will start identifying those emotions that are coming up before you react and unintentionally create a shadow. The challenge, of course, is you do not work in a bubble. You operate in the ecosystem of your workplace. In the next chapter, I want to help you to understand the balance that is needed to create that optimal performance within the workplace.

---

[*] Brown, Brené. (2015) Rising Strong. Penguin Random House UK.

CHAPTER FOUR

YOU CANNOT OUTSOURCE MENTAL HEALTH – IT IS YOUR SONG

I can remember if it was yesterday, the first rehearsal for *My Fair Lady* with the Fabulous Nobodies Theatre Company. Our Musical Director began our warm-up by getting us to sing 'Amazing Grace' together. Now granted, given it was musical theatre we could all sing in tune and we knew the song. But we did not know each other. The first time around it was a stock standard singing of the melody. Then he challenged us to create whatever harmonies we wanted. Not being so confident with harmonies, I sang the melody. But what an amazing sound we created! Someone would always lead the way with a harmony, and others would pick that up or build with another. It took my breath away, and this became a ritual at the beginning of every rehearsal—the richness of the song built over time. While we waited for the Musical Director to arrive, we would break into song. It was OUR song.

A sense of coming together as one before we got stuck into the hard work of the rehearsal.

Singing a song together is a great way of thinking about what culture can do for people. When we are 'new' we have to learn the song. Because of our underlying need to fit in, if we aren't comfortable about singing, we may stand in the back and just mouth the words. We can then at least look like we fit in. When we know the words, we sing along. Quietly at first. For those of us who aren't confident singers, this is as good as it gets. Some of us may never get the hang of the song and will choose to leave. Some might come in confidently but sing off tune. The looks from others soon tell us we aren't hitting the notes and we will adjust or go back to silent mouthing. Now and again, someone is so oblivious that they keep singing out of tune despite looks from others. It takes the Musical Director tapping them on the shoulder to help them realise they don't fit into the song. Those of us who are more confident, or have an adventurous spirit, might lead the way with harmonies that others soon follow. When singing a song together, everyone knows their parts. There are natural leaders and followers, and it works.

A song sung only with the melodic line can sound okay but can be monotonous, and not so exciting for the listener or the singers. But sung with multiple harmonies that change and build a song over time is beyond beautiful. And the feeling you get being part of producing that sound—now that is magical!

So too is the feeling when you understand how the workplace works at an underlying level—the melody- and then confidently strike a harmony—a new project or a different approach to solving a problem—which aligns with the underlying melody.

An organisation unlocks performance when it conducts a multi-layered harmonious choir.

Imagine though, in this choir if you take a break from singing to listen to an expert musician who wants to teach you some important components of singing together. But everything they are teaching is in a different genre. It's contemporary rock when you are used to rhythm and blues. While you are learning this, you are enjoying it, and it makes sense. But then you go back to work on the 'real' song, and you can't do what the expert taught you because the song of the organisation is rhythm and blues. You will always be pulled back to the song that your team is singing.

The current approach to mental health in too many organisations is similar to bringing in the expert musician. The external expert can teach you all sorts of interesting things. But when you go back to work, you will revert to the song of the organisation. If you want to build a mentally strong and healthy team that consistently performs, then mental health cannot just be a 'program' in the workplace. You cannot outsource it to someone who does not know the song or the genre. It's *your* song.

In past chapters, you delved into the pressures of the macro external environment and the micro understanding of mental health at an individual level. Then you have explored how interactions between yourself and others impact mental health through shadow talk, influenced by the classrooms inside your heads. Now it is time to look at the song of the organisation, where shadow talk is amplified because multiple shadows are being cast at an individual level under an overarching shadow of the organisation or your own department's song.

How does the cultural 'song' you create as a leader contribute to building or challenging mental health? How easily can people learn your song, and how do you enable them to build harmonies? The concept of culture is a difficult one for many—Adding in the concept of culture contributing to people's mental health, or not, can be rather daunting. Still, it's an important part of the equation we need to unpack in this chapter.

Corporate and government workplaces are increasingly employing health and wellbeing managers, suggesting that organisations are paying attention to the current conversation on mental health and have concerns about the implications for their workplaces.

From my experience, listening to presentations on what companies are doing, there is a significant focus on:
1. understanding mental health (although the focus is often understanding mild forms of mental illnesses NOT mental health for all)
2. responding when someone is in crisis (mental health first aid training is proliferating)
3. getting everyone to look after their mental health (the best of what I have seen).

Whatever the program, senior managers often look to the 'expert' to solve this issue as a sidebar to the main game of delivery. The programs then ultimately have a message of it's up to you as individuals to be resilient, using the tools we have given you, but we will support you individually if you are struggling.

At the same time, safety regulators are turning their focus to whether the work environment is psychologically safe.

They are asking whether:
• demands are reasonable
• people can safely raise issues without it being detrimental to their career at that workplace
• bullying and harassment are managed effectively
• conflict is solved effectively.

My advice is to get ahead of the curve. An individually focused mental health program is not enough. Likewise, you do not want safety regulators starting to dictate their view of psychologically safe workplaces. This is like having the expert musician who does not fully understand your organisation telling you the song to sing, despite not working for your organisation. If you wait for the 'expert musician', you will become reactive to a risk of reputation damage or prosecution from a regulator, rather than maximising the opportunity to build performance.

> *The responsibility at an individual level to look after mental and physical health will always be primary. But if we can understand how the workplace influences mental health for better or worse, we can build a mentally healthy culture that unlocks performance.*

Remember how shadow talk affects the individual? At an organisational level, that shadow is cast everywhere when people are feeling unsafe. If people do not have clarity of what they need to do, how well they are doing and do not feel safe to raise concerns, the classrooms inside people's heads turn negative and loud. If you think that mental health is a program you can outsource to the 'expert', then you are not maximising performance. People will not be their best when shadow talk is deafening.

The good news is, it is not as scary as you might think. I'll help you to:
- unpack how culture—your song—is formed
- understand what a mentally healthy culture could look like
- learn how you can influence this every day in how you lead, how you design your teams and workloads, and how you manage and recognise performance
- find the balance between getting individuals to own their mental health and owning the work environment as a leader.

If people are the key to success in your organisation, then you need to become the musical director that leads the choir in the song of your choosing.

———

Culture – What is *our* song?

Culture is the result of two laws of nature:
- *Safety in numbers*—those who are not sure will sing like others around them, so they look like they belong.
- *Survival of the fittest*—survival of those that can learn and build on harmonies of a song—those who create brilliant harmonies are recognised, those who sing out of tune or try to dominate the song get asked to change behaviour or leave. But the song remains.

Intentionally or not, as a leader you have chosen a song and are shaping the culture your teams operate within, because of the way you behave, the way you interact and what is going on in the classroom inside your head.

Before you run for the doors because you think cannot sing, let alone be a Musical Director, let's unpack culture so you can appreciate the simple ways you shape how people around you behave.

As humans, we look for social clues to understand how we fit in, blend or influence a particular setting. If there is no actual rule book—or songbook, we watch the people around us and learn from them what is acceptable.

Figure Seven is a simple version of the layers of the song that build culture.

FIGURE SEVEN

How culture is formed from the heart of the leader's values

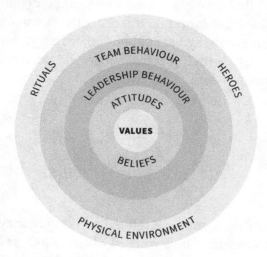

Your values (what you are truly passionate about when it all boils down to it) is you as the Director choosing the type of song. How those values and passion play out in how you behave in front of others results in a harmonious song, a stock standard melodic song or discord. It is up to you.

I will explain this concept with a greenfield company, how it builds over time from the core of the song to the outer layers— the multiple harmonies, or discord. I am going to go to extremes and apologise for leaning on a stereotype of merchant bankers in the process.

Values

As a merchant banker, I am setting up my own investment company. While I have not necessarily thought deeply about my dearest held values, money is the thing that I value more than anything else. I may say I care about other things, but money is what I am always thinking about making. Making money is my core value, my passion.

————

Attitudes and beliefs

Without realising it, my core value of making money drives my attitudes and beliefs. The strongest of those beliefs is 'I will be happy when I make my initial target, be that $10m, $100m or $1b. Of course, I am never happy with that first hurdle and become addicted to the chase. This focus on money then drives my attitudes. I am more comfortable associating with other people who have money, and I believe that if anyone puts their mind to it, they can make money.

————

Behaviour

Those ingrained attitudes and beliefs then drive my behaviour. I buy expensive clothes and cars, I live in an expensive suburb, and I have an office at a prestigious address. As I expand my business, attitudes and beliefs influence who I hire. I am hunting for those that are as hungry for money as myself. I am recruiting people into the team; one arrives in a Toyota and the other a Porsche. No disrespect to the people owning Toyotas but I am going to employ the Porsche owner. They already understand what money's all about, and therefore I want them in my team. Unless the Porsche owner thinks that owning a Porsche is enough and is not hungry! My behaviour represents me singing the song on my own.

————

Team behaviour

As I start to expand my team, I am expecting to see behaviours around me that are similar to my own, making me feel comfortable. These behaviours made me successful, and I want to see them repeated in my team. Hence, the culture starts to take shape. Everyone starts to learn what I value—they are learning the song. Therefore, they are going to behave similarly, because that enables them to remain in this job, get the bonus or get promoted. When my team is small, we start just singing the melody together.

————

Heroes, rituals, physical environment

As I grow that business, I cannot control everyone that I am recruiting, and I cannot watch the behaviours of every single person. So, I need to create the next two layers of the song, which is about the rituals I create, the heroes that get created because of the behaviours I celebrate and the physical environment I create. These are strong cues to those wanting to learn the song quickly so they can fit in, then stand out as leaders of new harmonies that help me expand my business further.

If you want to come and see my organisation, you will find us at one of the most prestigious addresses in the city. I choose to make sure when you walk into my workplace; you see a sense of money in everything. From the opulence of the furniture to the original artwork on the walls. When I am taking you to the boardroom that has amazing views over the city, you will see all the awards that we have won. I am giving you the sense that you are in the presence of success.

When you observe my organisation, you will see the key rituals. I will implement rituals that reinforce how much I love money and why money is important. For example, we will have a locked fridge of Bollinger or rare Dom Perignon. Each time we make the next ten million dollars, someone rings a bell and everyone cheers. We know that we are going to pop that next bottle of champagne. Of course, when we do this, there is a celebration of who achieved this next milestone. Those that are named again and again become the heroes. They get reward after reward and promotion after promotion. Everything screams money above all else.

Over time, I may not even be in the office that often. But, my design of the physical environment, who I have recruited, promoted and recognised and what we celebrate clearly displays to everyone 'the song'. If you want to fit in here, make me money. The harmonious song is being sung, and I'll come and listen to it now and again to make sure I am happy everyone is still in tune.

An extreme example, but it gives you a sense of how we form a culture in the first instance. If you create a business from scratch as I did in my earlier consulting days, your values as a leader will influence everything about how you create this culture. When I was setting out with a business partner to build this business, we were clear on the culture we wanted. We then went about creating it—we hired people who understood the genre and could learn the song quickly, then expand it with harmonies.

The conscious choice of influencing these layers gets you the culture you want. The unconscious growing and running of a business gets you the culture you deserve.

I have worked from the inside to the outside in explaining how culture is formed. I now want to take you to the inside from the outside. When I come into a workplace to determine the culture, I assess what I experience, not what I am told by management. I observe the physical environment, the rituals, the heroes, and typical behaviours.

It is an expectation that listed companies expressly state their values. Yet, in my consulting experience, many employees roll their eyes at these stated values. It is not what they experience, and this is where discord starts.

It's what I am seeing in action that gives me the best indication of what song you are singing and what I need to do to thrive in this setting:
- How you behave when under pressure helps me understand the core values that drive you
- The behaviours you choose to ignore tell me what you truly value, as much as the behaviours you reward—particularly those behaviours you would ignore in those who deliver strong financial results
- What the environment looks like shows me what pride there is and what is considered important to performance.

It's also the people that you are exalting and promoting. If the team see you encourage someone who makes you money but does not treat people respectfully through the process, then

PRACTICAL STEPS:

First glance assessment of culture

Be a tourist in your town. Walk through your workplace and reflect on behaviours you observe over the next month to form a view of what the underlying culture at your workplace is. In doing so, consider these questions:

What do you see in the physical environment? Is it tired and worn or in good condition? Are notice boards out of date or full of new photos and information for people? Is it untidy or tidy?

What behaviours do you see? Are people smiling and interacting? Are they looking rushed and harried? Is there an energetic buzz, a manic buzz or dead quiet?

Observe what rituals people seem to follow consistently. For example, what appears to be accepted start and finish times? What do people wear? Are meetings always starting and finishing on time? Does everyone come to meetings? How often do people get recognised for their contribution? How do people deal with conflict?

Ask people questions about heroes. What do you think you need to do to get a big bonus? To get promoted? Who is most influential in this organisation?

The answers to these questions start to give you an insight into the song your organisation or your team is singing. Now you need to take the next step and work out whether this song is mentally healthy for your team.

the message the team gets loud and clear is that respect does not matter. Just make money. If despite the pressures of work, when someone is unwell, everyone stops to support, this speaks volumes of caring for others being at the heart of the culture.

As a manager at a senior level, it's easy to think that culture is set at an organisational level, and you cannot change that. But you, as a leader, no matter how many teams you've got underneath you, create a subculture.

Think about this as taking a subset of the choir to teach them a harmony, then getting them to join back into the overall song to influence its direction. Stop and think, 'What are the rituals that I have, what is the environment and who are the people that I am recognising and celebrating in the teams?' That is what is giving the best signals to other people about what is important in your teams. If you want the best performance, you need to get into the driver's seat of creating your part of the song—your culture.

Use the questions on the 'first glance assessment of culture' exercise as a prompter to help you reflect on what you can do to start shaping the culture of your team. Yes, the culture of the organisation is bigger than you, but as a leader, you are at a crossroads for choice here in what you want to do to get the best performance out of your teams. Influence the song in your place then watch it build from there.

———

Mentally healthy workplaces – Is the song harmonious?

If you have been in a senior role for an extended period, you would have had enough exposure to health and safety requirements to understand your role in looking after people's physical safety. The individual has to take care of their physical health, but as an employer, you cannot allow plant, equipment or processes to endanger their lives. This role is the same for mental health. The individual still owns their mental health, but you as a senior manager own the culture or the song of the team or organisation. This culture may or may not be mentally healthy. It may be out of tune and not creating the brilliant song you want, but you are on the hook to create a psychologically safe work environment.

An individual will perform at their best if they feel confident in the song of the team or organisation, and the song matches their style.

If your organisation only runs programs focused on people looking after their mental health, but they work in a culture which is not mentally healthy, then this will not get the best from the team. It will not create a harmonious song that unlocks performance.

A harmonious song does not mean that conflict or disagreement are not allowed—this is people walking around on eggshells. Everyone trying to sing the one melody with no harmonies allowed.

A healthy culture is a harmonious, layered song. It can express a range of different emotions and different intensities of these emotions. Imagine conflict as a rising crescendo of noise with unusual harmonies. Still, the voices work with each other to shift from angry chords to excited, energised or perhaps even joyful or calm chords. The different emotions in the song are the same as the harmonies. It makes the song interesting. It keeps the singers involved and working together. Conflicting views, which I prefer to think about as cognitive diversity, bring out creativity. As long as the team feel safe to voice these views and the underlying premise is to sing together, you can create a mentally healthy workplace. Conflict is normal, but unresolved conflict is unhealthy to both the individual and the organisation. It is not singing harmoniously, and no one is doing anything to get the song back on track.

Let's use the fundamental principles of the mental health pie to look at what creates a mentally healthy workplace.

- **Connection:** If I feel like I belong, and feel safe, then I can focus on the job at hand with a happy dose of oxytocin. If I do not feel these things, the negative shadow talk will overtake, and cortisol will flood my body. *I will not be my best for you.*
- **Curiosity:** If I work in an environment where failure is consistently seen as a way of learning, and everyone around me remains curious about what we can learn, then I can get into a curious state too and help solve the problems we face with a happy dose of dopamine. If failure means criticism, my cortisol will get triggered as I will feel under threat. *I will not be my best for you.*
- **Contribution:** If I feel that what I am doing helps the team or organisation and I am valued for this, then this will feel great with a happy dose of serotonin, and I will keep working hard for you. If I am not recognised for my hard work and do not feel valued, I will begin to worry about my job security, and the cortisol will come into play again. *I will not be my best for you.*

Underlying all this is the premise that;

> *In a mentally healthy workplace, the team can collectively say 'We have been seen, we have been heard, and we matter'.*

To kickstart your thinking, Figure Eight shows what people are saying in a mentally healthy workplace.

FIGURE EIGHT

What people say in a mentally healthy workplace

Connection

- I feel like I belong, I can be myself and know I am accepted.
- I'm part of a team.
- My boss gets me.
- I have people I can ask for advice and support from
- We treat everyone with dignity and respect, regardless of the circumstances.
- I get recognised for what I do.
- I have a friend or two in the workplace who I can be completely vulnerable with and who truly care for me.
- I feel safe raising issues of concern and know we will solve them together.

Curiosity

- I am given good challenges that help me think differently and keep learning.
- I feel safe to ask questions and make mistakes in my learning.
- I feel safe raising alternative ideas to solve problems.
- I know change will occur, but the way I'm involved in that change keeps me learning along the way about what's going on.

Contribution

- I've got clarity on what I need to do and how it relates to the broader goals or vision of the organisation.
- I'm capable and have the capacity to do that job.
- I get regular feedback that helps me understand how well I am contributing.
- I am valued for the job I do.
- I am listened to – my opinion matters.

Let's flip these statements into a diagnostic for you. Use the questions in Table Two to reflect on what you are consciously or unconsciously creating in the workplace. For each focus area, there are yes or no questions. Once you have answered the questions, circle those to which you responded 'No'. These become your action list to create a mentally healthy workplace.

You can see it's not rocket science, but it does take focus.

Regulators want to see organisations manage risk to prevent mental illness attributed to the workplace. You want to maximise the opportunity to connect to retain talent and build performance.

TABLE TWO   Is your workplace mentally healthy?

Connection	
	• Do I know the personal background of each person in the team?
	• Do I know what motivates each person in the team? What recognition receives the best response? What their ambitions are and why?
	• Am I consciously taking actions each week to motivate my direct team at a personal level?
	• Do I see the team working effectively together?
	• Do team members come together to solve not criticise when things go wrong?
	• When someone is sick, do I stay connected with them during time away from work? And does the team?
	• When I have 'failed' the team or someone in the team do I acknowledge it?

TABLE TWO Is your workplace mentally healthy?

Curiosity	• Have I got each person periodically just outside their comfort zone to learn?
	• Am I giving them time to rebound from learning before putting them outside the comfort zone again?
	• Am I personally able to remain curious?
	• Am I regularly discussing 'failures' as a team to work out what we can learn and do differently as a team?
	• Am I comfortable responding to the constant change in the workplace?
	• Am I consciously triggering curiosity in the team during times of change?
Contribution	• Are there clear position descriptions for every role?
	• Has every role got measurable KPIs that link to others in the team, to mine, and the organisations?
	• Can everyone see each other's KPIs?
	• Are those KPIs achievable within the hours people are employed?
	• Is everyone capable of doing the job I need them to do?
	• Can I measure what I expect of them?
	• Am I regularly providing feedback on what they do?
	• Is this feedback encouraging AND rewarding?
	• Am I consciously taking action each week to make sure every team member genuinely feels valued for their contribution?

If you are in a space where you've got people complaining that your workplace is not mentally healthy, internally or externally, then you are in a whole other world of pain. You are dealing with problems, not opportunity. Get ahead of the curve. Start taking action using the above list to guide you.

———

What if I am not confident at directing music?

The larger and older the organisation, the more influential the culture can feel. Regardless of seniority, many managers have had conversations with me over the years around the view they cannot change 'the organisation'. They are right. One person cannot change an organisation but imagine if every manager took accountability for creating the mentally healthy culture of their team. My recommendation to managers is always to start with your direct reports. Create the harmonious song there and hold them to account to do the same for their teams. Then talk to another manager at the same level as you and help them do the same. Have you ever seen the video 'First Follower: Leadership Lessons from Dancing Guy' by Derek Sivers? If you haven't, google it. It is fascinating to watch how one person dancing on their own is just some weird random dancer. The key person is the first follower. The person who is prepared to join when there is not yet safety in numbers.

I experimented with this theory in a role at Coles with a room of approximately 200 people. Now granted these were Coles senior retail managers who are inherently energetic and extroverted. But it was fascinating. When I was introduced, I danced onto the stage with music, then kept dancing. I had not warned my team I was going to do this, and they were looking at each other thinking I had been drinking. Perhaps more so because I am not a good dancer. I had engineered the first three people to gradually join me on stage—although the first person did leave me hanging for some time before she jumped in as the first follower! What I had not expected, but perhaps hoped for was what happened next. One by one, the people in the room started standing up and dancing. Then more joined in, and there began a great conversation on what leadership is all about. You start a movement and others will follow.

The key message is, do not wait for the 'organisation' to lead the way. Accept it is your role as a leader to shape the culture of the department you run. Then by example, you will naturally influence other teams. The engagement and subsequent performance will have people wanting to join you—and other managers emulate you.

You have control of how things operate within your team. You can create the right structure, the right work for people, the correct combination of skill sets, and the environment to trigger connection, curiosity and contribution. You have the ability to make your team feel that they have been seen, they have been heard, and they matter. You can own and learn your shadow talk and help the rest of the team understand this too. So, you can create the harmonious song that is a mentally healthy workplace.

Who owns which part of the performance of the song?

You own the song, and you are the musical director when it comes to the culture of your team. It is your job to be clear with your team about what you need them to do to make the song work. It is your job to give feedback and coach to build confidence when they aren't singing the way they need to. It's your job to help guide them when you see the blind panic of 'I do not know the song or my harmony'. The individual needs to take accountability for learning and performing their contribution to the song Likewise, the individual has to own their realisation that if this song is not for them, they can protect their mental health by moving teams or organisations to find a song that suits their skills.

When you see a team member suddenly slide to red, it is also important to not view work as the only contributor—or a contributor at all. Remember, a severe mental or physical illness can strike people unexpectedly. Ultimately the individual does need to own their slide down the continuum, the same as the individual owns what they do to respond to a physical illness affecting their body. However, when you see a team member slide down the continuum, it is valuable to refer to the mentally healthy workplace checklist and identify whether anything needs to change to help that person become more connected, curious and contributing to help them return to green.

An excellent way to find the balance is by thinking about physical health. You are not likely to ask everyone in your team how much they are exercising, sleeping and eating. You might be happy to talk with them collectively about the importance of their physical health. You may share stories and encourage them to do the same, so you build an awareness of looking after physical health. You would also likely look at the physical environment and patterns of behaviour that could interfere with physical health. The person who falls asleep at their desk, who is steadily gaining—or losing— weight or someone who is continuously taking sick leave are clear signs someone is not in good physical health. Individuals need to own their physical health, but you can encourage physical health in discussion, set up an environment that promotes physical health and address concerns with them. You can also do this with mental health. Encourage 'mental health' shares at the beginning of team meetings to bring awareness of what each person needs in that week. Maybe sharing an emoji which represents the feelings on that day. This sharing creates much laughter but also good reflections on how best to support or celebrate with each other. Look at the work design and processes and how the team deal with pressure to create a mentally healthy workplace. Look out for changes in behaviour that signal someone sliding into the orange and call it out before they slip into red. Own the song. Get the individual to own their crucial contribution to the song.

———

Key things to remember

- At the heart of any culture is the actual not stated values of those that lead it.
- Our teams will judge us on the behaviours they see of us not what we assert is our culture—this is intent versus impact on scale.
- This culture is like a song the organisation or business unit that you lead sings. It is discordant, stock stand melody up to multi-layer harmony depending on YOUR behaviours and the behaviours YOU influence in the organisation.

- To create that harmonious song—a mentally healthy workplace—where people thrive, you need to look at how you build connection, contribution and curiosity.

As leaders, we have to hold this song in our teams. We cannot outsource it to someone running a mental health and wellbeing program. We have to own it as much as we have to own our shadow from Chapter Three.

Do not take the easy path of outsourcing and ticking a box for mental health. Yes, the programs are valuable, and teams typically respond well, 'in the moment'. But if this program sings a different song to the culture at large, it will not sustain even over the short term, let alone the medium to long term.

You unlock performance when you own the song of culture for your organisation and deliberately shape behaviours.

Use the mentally healthy workplace checklist in this chapter to help you think deeply about what song you are creating in your workplace.

People still need the reminders and useful tips that health and wellbeing programs offer. But they also need to feel that they fit in—*are singing the right song* and can genuinely add value—*build exciting harmonies together*—in the organisation. So 'Musical Director', read on to the next chapter to build confidence in your resilience for this journey on which you are about to embark.

CHAPTER FIVE

CONNECTING TO SELF

I found myself as the frog in boiling water several years back. I did not appreciate it at the time, but I had gone into orange without realising it. It sounds ridiculous to articulate this now, but I would be driving home from work in tears more often than not. I wasn't sleeping well. I was getting tense about most things, which did not seem abnormal at the time. I was used to the level of tension in the workplace, the negativity, the breakdown in relationships. I was so determined to keep pushing through, I had not been able to take stock and realise the impact on me. And the effect I was having on others because of my state. I had slipped further down the mental health continuum than I ever want to slide again, and it took a long time to get myself back to green.

What I do know from this time is that while I would not want to wish that experience on anyone, I am wiser and stronger for having processed what happened. It enabled me to grow as a leader and increase my drive to help others in understanding the mental health spectrum. I am aware that one of the most critical skills for anyone wanting to manage their mental health proactively, is to connect with yourself—to learn to read what is going on with you physically and emotionally and to alter your behaviour to influence your health.

In the previous chapters, we looked at the external working environment and the risks it poses. We looked at what happens internally as our brain processes information and releases chemicals that influence us, sometimes without us consciously realising. We also reflected on how that classroom inside our and other people's heads create shadow talk that is not always helpful. And how this shadow talk is amplified by the 'song'—*culture*—of the organisation.

Now that you have a grounding in the basics of mental health, it is time to get into a much stronger self-reflection mode to truly understand where you are and have been on the continuum and how well you have baked your mental health pie. You cannot pass GO as a leader until you have sorted out your mental health pie.

Often, when I help a team, the response from the manager in the first one-to-one discussion is a deflection away from them to focus on the team concerns or needs. I am going to challenge you on that view. Hopefully, because of what you have learned already with regards to the continuum of mental health, you can recognise that every single one of us is vulnerable. If you do not consciously work on your mental health continuously, you are not going to perform at your best, and you will not get the best performance from your team nor be the role model that can help them solve their problems.

*If you do not consciously learn to connect
to yourself by stepping back—to observe and
influence your thought patterns, behaviours and
emotions—your overactive thinking brain with these
wonderful survival chemicals can override, leading
to poor mental health and poor performance.*

You need to be able to learn new pathways to make sure that you are strengthening the 'muscles' in the brain, that look after your mental health. Even if you are not entirely convinced right now, and think you are mentally strong, life happens. Regardless of who you are, life throws unexpected curveballs at you—it could be a new boss, a changing work environment, the sudden death of a loved one, or even an issue with your physical health—they all impact on your mental health. Use this chapter to learn how to connect with yourself on an ongoing basis and learn to read the signs of your health or lack thereof.

We know from Chapter Two that contribution, curiosity and connecting to self and others are the key factors to being mentally healthy. In this chapter, we are going to explore the foundation ingredient of the mental health pie, connecting to self. It is through this awareness that you can decide how to create the rest of your pie in subsequent chapters.

We will explore how to:
• assess yourself on the continuum
• connect to your physical self
• connect to your psychological self
• build habits that keep the pie fresh
• bring yourself back to green when you have slipped into yellow.

By the end of this chapter, you will have a good selection of practical tools in your kit for mental health that you can then help others with too.

Have you got your oxygen mask on?

While it is repeated every time you fly, to the point you may not even register it, the airlines always remind you, in the case of an emergency, to fit your oxygen mask before helping others. Connecting to self is like putting your oxygen mask on first. If you cannot breathe, then you are not going to be useful to anyone else.

You need to build up the muscle of periodically stopping and assessing what is going on in that classroom inside your head. What are the thoughts? Feelings? Physical reactions? And what is happening in the environment that might further impact these? All those things help you identify where you might be sitting on the continuum. That ability to stop and reflect on what is happening right now is essential. This ability is what connecting to self is all about. There are some simple assessments of both lag and lead indicators that help you connect to yourself and understand where you are on the continuum. You can use different components of the mental health pie to help shift back to green if your connection with self indicates you need to act.

Assessing your energy level

0–2
Am I exhausted at the end of every day?
Am I falling asleep on the couch?
Am I dragging myself out of bed in the mornings?
Am I not sleeping well?
Do I need a pile of caffeine to get me through the day?

5–6
Am I feeling calm and in control most of the time?
Am I taking regular breaks from intense conversations to stop and think?
Am I regularly doing things that re-energise me?

9–10
Am I full speed or zero every day?
Am I not stopping to reflect each day?
Am I always talking at a million miles an hour?
Am I getting a 'high' with what I am delivering and keep pushing myself?

Lag indicator 1

What is your energy level right now?

You are looking for flagging or manic energy as warning signs. Stop and ask yourself the self-connection questions in Figure Nine regularly, to understand your energy levels right now and work out where you are on a scale of 0–10. Persistent low energy or unsustainable high energy are indicators you have slipped into yellow. You should aim to stay within a reasonable range of 5 and not spend time close to 0 or 10 for too long before finding the balance again.

Lag indicator 2

How often are negative emotions bubbling to the surface?

We talked about emotions briefly in Chapter Three. We all feel different emotions at different times. But if you think back to last week or the previous month, are those negative emotions coming up too often or too intensely or hanging around too long? If you experience a negative emotion and can pause, identify it, work out what that emotion might be telling you and take reasonable action because of it, you are comfortably in green. If you are finding yourself experiencing intense negative emotions most days, or a feeling comes up and keeps persisting long past the day, that is a good indicator you have slipped into yellow.

Lag indicator 3

What is the classroom inside your head right now?

An overthinking brain can get stuck in loops. So, check-in with yourself with these questions:
- What past or future conversations keep playing around in your head?
- What is the critical voice in the classroom saying to you right now?
- How often is the critical voice in the classroom dominating?
- What is distracting you from being present right now?
- What worries or concerns or problems are keeping you awake at night?

A persistent negative narrative in that classroom is a good indicator that you have slipped into yellow and need to act.

Lag indicator 4

What is happening or about to occur in the external environment right now that is increasing pressure for you?

You do not exist in a vacuum, and it is often an external event that can trigger you to slip into yellow. The more aware you are of these factors, the better you can prepare your body and brain.

When you say you are fine, I want you to remember the poor frog in the water. Changes in the environment will impact you. Even a positive change, such as buying a house or organising a major holiday, can still affect your mental health. Stay aware of what is changing in your environment that could impact you.

You need to work on understanding your shifts of energy, emotion, classroom voices and environment regularly—this is connecting to self.

If you are not increasing self-awareness about where you are on the continuum, then you can easily slip into yellow or orange without even realising it, because you are just on the treadmill of life.

What was that saying, 'Be alert, not alarmed'? That is what connecting to self is all about. Use the questions in each of these lag indicators as a guide to connecting to self.

If this feels like just another thing to add to your long 'to-do' list, then it will not work. You cannot afford not to create the time because the further down the continuum you go, the longer you'll take to recover. But it doesn't take long, to stop and think about these questions. And it takes less time to check in regularly with yourself than the time it takes to recover from being in orange. Remember, it is normal for anyone to shift between green and yellow. But if you persist in that yellow space, it becomes the norm, and you can slip further down to orange without noticing.

Please note, if you are particularly concerned about negative thoughts, energy levels and emotions, I recommend you go on to the Beyond Blue site, where there is a valid clinical tool for anxiety and depression. It does not take long, and while it does not give a diagnosis, it will give you a score with recommendations about whether you need some further intervention or to have a conversation with your doctor about what help you need right now.

———

What do you do with where you are?

Lag indicator 'check-in' questions are a great way of connecting to self in the moment. It is much more powerful though to stop and look at lead indicators periodically, which can tell you how at risk you are of sliding into orange. The best way to do this is by assessing yourself against the ingredients of the mental health pie.

Evaluate yourself right now on each of the different parts of the pie. Figure Ten contains activities that could be in each of those areas of the pie, to help you to determine where you might fit on the scale.

I want you to rate each of the four areas of the pie from zero to five:
- **0** – I am doing nothing in that part of the pie at the moment.
- **1** – I have just started an activity in this section of the pie.
- **2** – I have a few activities I am testing out.
- **3** – I have a reasonable number of activities in this section but my habit often slips.
- **4** – I have a strong habit or two in this section of the pie and others I am working on.
- **5** – I have got a range of things in this section of the pie built into habit.

The suggestions that could be in each of those areas of the pie, will help you to determine where you might fit on the scale.

FIGURE TEN

The Mental Health Pie ingredients

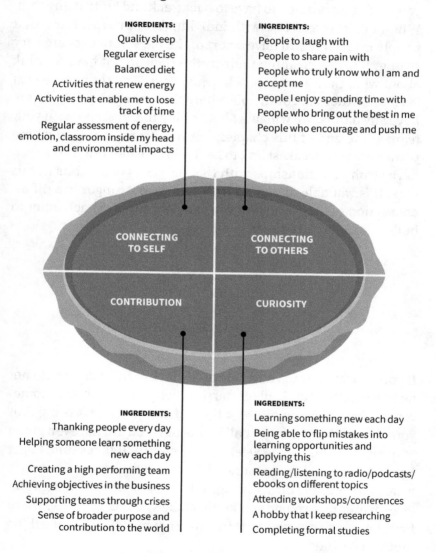

INGREDIENTS:
Quality sleep
Regular exercise
Balanced diet
Activities that renew energy
Activities that enable me to lose track of time
Regular assessment of energy, emotion, classroom inside my head and environmental impacts

INGREDIENTS:
People to laugh with
People to share pain with
People who truly know who I am and accept me
People I enjoy spending time with
People who bring out the best in me
People who encourage and push me

CONNECTING TO SELF

CONNECTING TO OTHERS

CONTRIBUTION

CURIOSITY

INGREDIENTS:
Thanking people every day
Helping someone learn something new each day
Creating a high performing team
Achieving objectives in the business
Supporting teams through crises
Sense of broader purpose and contribution to the world

INGREDIENTS:
Learning something new each day
Being able to flip mistakes into learning opportunities and applying this
Reading/listening to radio/podcasts/ebooks on different topics
Attending workshops/conferences
A hobby that I keep researching
Completing formal studies

The reality is that, at any one point in time, one part of that pie may not be as strong as another because of personal preferences. Or external circumstances have wiped half the pie's habits from you, and you are going to have to backtrack and build it up again. When I do this exercise with individuals or groups, I find that people invariably will have a part of the pie where they are very strong. It is like cleaning their teeth—they do not have to think about what they are doing. They just do it. And then there is at least one other part of the pie where they recognise they do not have any habits. We will talk about doing this exercise with your team at the end of this chapter, but it is useful to reflect where you assess your weakest link to be. Then consider others that you have strong relationships with that do have good habits in this area. It is valuable to pair up with someone stronger in a different section of the pie so that you can help support each other to build the right ingredients.

Not enough ingredients?

If you look at your pie and pale at the lack of ingredients, do not be overwhelmed and put off starting. You just have to start somewhere. Just take one bite at a time. It can feel like it is big, but you do not have to conquer all in one day. You are not even going to overcome this in one week or one month. It takes time to get habits embedded. You just need to start somewhere. Start with what you see as the most manageable steps to take, the things that already interest you or you know make you feel good. Go there first, because once you start to build that muscle up, you will be motivated to add others.

If you start with one of the hardest things, you are never going to get there. You might not be that interested in, or find it hard to find time for walking, but enjoy connecting with people. Great! Then start with connecting with a friend, then as this habit builds, you can suggest walking when catching up, rather than sitting down over a coffee. That is a simple way to increase the ingredients.

———

How do I connect to my physical self?

Your physical self and your psychological self are entirely inter-connected. Chances are if you are not feeling mentally well, it means that you are not completely physically well and vice versa. In my experience, this first step of connecting with your physical self is often the easiest one for senior managers to start with as it typically fits in their comfort zone.

I do not need to convince you that your physical health is vital to ongoing performance in a senior role. I love the concept though of the corporate athlete—of particular interest because my husband is a sports physiotherapist, involved with elite athletes. I have seen first-hand how disciplined elite athletes are about their rest and recovery as much as they are about their training and their peak performance on the day.

Athletes have ingrained in them that there is a point in time at which they must be their best. But to be able to peak at their best when needed, they need the training to build up to that point, and they need to do this with a rhythm of recovery and rest. They understand the rhythmic cycle of train, recover, rest. Train, recover, rest, performance, recover, rest, train, recover, rest.

In the corporate world, most people do not seem to understand that cycle. It is almost like managers think they need to be at peak performance all the time. Yes, the 'camera' is always on senior managers when they are at work. However, you need to recognise that work can't always be at peak performance. You need to talk loudly about how you rest and recover so 'the camera' gets the complete picture of what it takes to sustain senior roles. You have got to be able to think about that balance. And tell your team how you keep that balance to role model the behaviour that everyone needs to adopt.

Connecting with your physical self is stopping and asking yourself where you sit in the ingredients for your physical self and taking simple actions to look after your sleep, exercise and food requirements.

Sleep

Sleep is so important. Our brains are 'working' when we are sleeping. They are in recovery mode.

I know too many people who like to boast about how little rest they 'need'. Yes, different people are born with varying sleep needs depending on how efficiently they sleep. Still, I believe that some people—particularly senior managers—kid themselves about how little sleep they need, and they become the frog in the water. But imagine how much more productive you could be with a good sleep routine.

Arianna Huffington of Huffington Post fame is an excellent example of a convert to the value of more rather than less sleep. She too fell prey to surviving on little sleep until she had a complete break-down[*]. It is valuable to take the lesson she learnt now rather than experiencing it personally.

---

[*] Huffington, A. ((2014). Thrive: The Third Metric to Redefining Success and Creating a Happier Life. Harmony Books, Random House. USA.

I like to think about the brain as full of filing cabinets. At the end of each day, from all the experiences we have had, the brain needs to determine which files it can discard and which files it should retain as useful memories or experiences that reinforce our view on life for our pattern-seeking brain. We need time for our minds to reorder themselves or the paperwork keeps piling up. The brain can cope for a while without filing but not over the long term. Remember, this is about connecting to the physical self. You need to keep checking in with your body and be honest with yourself. Is your sleep pattern truly maximising your energy?

Check-in regularly and ask yourself these questions:
- Are you keeping regular sleep and waking times?
- Have you got a good routine pre-bed so you can trigger your brain that it is time to sleep?
- Do you keep devices away from the bedroom?
- Can you completely darken your room to get the best sleep?
- Can you keep the bedroom cool, so you do not overheat?
- When you are extra tired, do you go to bed earlier rather than sleep in?

Food

The next ingredient to strengthen is eating well. I am not a dietitian, and I am not going to give you a whole pile of rules about what to eat or not eat. Every year it feels like a new diet appears that purports to be *the* diet. When it comes to food, we need to listen to, and connect with, our bodies more. The best piece advice I received was 'Do what works for you'. My build on this is to keep assessing your energy, emotions, classroom inside your head and environment, to identify relationships between how you are feeling and what you are eating. I know for myself that when I am tired, I do not make wise choices on what I eat (the chocolate calls). Making me more tired and affecting my sleep. And so, the cycle goes on if I do not connect with myself, recognise the loop and break it with the next ingredient, which is exercise.

Exercise

I have heard it said that exercise is the best anti-depressant in the world. In fact, 'exercise'—which I define as regular physical activity in the day that can get your heart rate up and keep it up—has both physical and psychological benefits. Those who can build exercise into habit appreciate the feeling of the endorphins released post-exercise. Here is another 'feel good' chemical from our brain. Our brain wants us to exercise given the benefits, so it provides us with a chemical that makes us feel good when we do it. Just like food, though, 'do what works for you'.

With the increased willingness for people to talk about their mental health, there have been high profile people in sports who have acknowledged their struggles with mental ill-health. These acknowledgements do not imply that exercising is not a protective factor against mental illness. It is a very important ingredient but only *one of many*. The impact on sports people reminds us of both the importance of building up every part of the pie and recognising the indiscriminate way that mental illness, like some serious physical illnesses, can hit us. As with diet, your best bet is building up the pie with physical activity that works for you.

The 'what works for you' motto likely means that if you have not already set up a discipline of exercise, you might need to experiment with different options before finding the right one for you. One of the tricks I have seen work effectively is linking exercise with a social connection. For example, going walking with your partner or close friend to debrief on issues regularly. Therefore, the exercise is incidental to the conversation. Or getting a dog who will keep reminding you to take them out.

In my coaching of executives in mental health, particularly males, it is more common than not that exercise is the strongest ingredient in the pie. Running and cycling appeared to be the most common forms of exercise. If you fall into this category, brilliant. Go back to the pie and make sure you balance this out with ingredients from other parts of the pie. The risk is an assumption that a run or cycle can clear your head every time, and you do not need other ingredients such as connection, contribution and curiosity. It is called the *Mental Health Pie* for a reason. You miss vital ingredients, and it will not work.

When you are doing a lot of travel, whether international or domestic, your rhythm or routine can get disrupted. I love the movie *Up in the Air* with George Clooney, which illustrates an extreme example of the importance of a travel routine. Clooney's character went to the extreme of even hiring the same car in every city to which he travelled. Now I am not suggesting you go to that extreme, but if you do travel regularly you need to recognise this risk and put in a ritual that works for you. For the places that I travel to frequently, I prefer to stay in the same hotel because I am familiar with *that* hotel, *that* gym and their services. Packing my gym gear then becomes a non-negotiable and I make sure that I have that time in the morning or the evening to run. The travel ritual maintains the habit.

Connecting with your physical self is being mindful of what you are doing to look after your body and listening to what your body is telling you. This mindful check-in is an important way of helping to prevent issues and picking them up when they occur. You will never be perfect, so be kind to yourself when you check-in. Recognise what has triggered the poor behaviour and take a simple action. Remember we are all human, and tomorrow is another day.

Because your physical and psychological selves are so interconnected, it can often be the classroom inside your head that is contributing to your physical routine not being where it needs to be.

So, when you are not in the right routine and are finding it hard to work out where to start, it is time to check-in with your psychological self.

———

How do I connect to my psychological self?

Talking about the psychological self might get a little uncomfortable for some people. Still, it is important to understand as much about the psychological side of ourselves as the physical side.

The four lag indicators at the beginning of the chapter are a useful starting point for checking in with your psychological self. Regularly checking in allows you to identify issues before they become significant problems. However, there is a more proactive method for checking in with your psychological self and keeping it in balance. The key way to connect to your psychological side proactively is through mindfulness. You have probably come across this term before. It is a bit of a buzzword at the moment— for good reason as we will see. For some, the term mindfulness is automatically connected to meditation and conjures an image of someone sitting cross-legged chanting *'Ommm'* repeatedly. But it is much broader than that.

The Oxford dictionary provides two definitions that are useful in understanding the value of mindfulness;

1. the quality or state of being conscious or aware of something;
2. a mental state achieved by focusing one's awareness on the present moment, while calmly acknowledging and accepting one's feelings, thoughts and bodily sensations.

Another way of thinking about mindfulness is stopping your animal brain from being caught up in past or future threats. In our busy world, it is easy to get caught in automatic mode where we do not stop and connect in with ourselves. Our identity can be wrapped up in our feelings, thoughts and bodily sensations. Dr Daniel Siegel's excellent book, *Mindsight**, explains the importance of being able to step away from the automatic nature of our brain and recognise that who we are is more than just our constant thinking, feeling and bodily sensations.

Mindfulness is a check-in to challenge the classroom inside your head, to give yourself a chance to settle the chatter and subsequent chemicals that are not helping you. It is an awareness of yourself. It brings you back to the present moment where you are not caught up in worry about the past or the future. It is vital to your mental health.

Two key mindfulness tools will help you build your psychological health:
- knowing how to maintain and restore your psychological energy
- building in regular perspective taking.

---

* Siegel, Daniel J. MD (2012) Mindsight – change your brain and your life. Scribe Publications Pty Ltd. London, UK.

How do I maintain and restore mental energy?

Are you an introvert or an extrovert? I am not talking about how confident or reserved you are in the crowd; I am talking about how you renew your energy. If your energy is low, what is the activity that you choose to bring it back up again? Does it involve being with people, or do you need time to yourself? For extreme extroverts, being with anyone replenishes their energy, while other extroverts may only gain energy from being with certain people. Strong introverts need time alone to recharge. You might be a little of both. The critical point is to recognise what environments recharge your battery effectively and efficiently. If you are connecting in effectively with yourself, and recognise your energy depleting, permit yourself to recharge with solitude or social activities. Whatever gets you enjoying the moment and forgetting about the past or future for a while. It enables the brain to feel safe—stopping the cortisol and releasing those happy chemicals.

Mihaly Csikszentmihalyi is an eminent psychologist who has done extensive research on the concept of 'flow'. Flow is completely losing all sense of time and worries around you because you are so completely engrossed in what you are doing at that point. He does not talk about it as a concept of happiness, per se, so much as mindfulness—of being utterly present 'in the moment'. Flow is an excellent way of recharging your psychological energy. Typically, when we are in flow, we are doing something that makes us feel confident or curious, something we enjoy or maybe something that makes us feel valued and appreciated. Being in flow triggers our serotonin and dopamine. If it is with others, it can also trigger oxytocin. It is also where the classroom inside our head ceases to exist—a fantastic space in which to live.

Is this familiar to you? Are there things you enjoy doing that have you entirely focused in the present moment?

For me it is on a horse, cantering along the beach on the Mornington Peninsula. I am not a brilliant rider, so a part of me is just concentrating on staying on the horse—no chance of a classroom in my head at that point. Another part of me is just enjoying sitting on this incredibly powerful animal in a beautiful setting, feeling the wind whipping across my face, and I am entirely present—nothing else matters at that time.

But flow is not restricted to non-work activities. It is valuable in a senior manager role where work is demanding to identify when you can get into flow with work.

> *While there will always be challenges in work that will drain you, knowing the tasks in work that put you in flow enables you to choose these activities at the right time to trigger the chemicals you need to keep the balance right.*

In a work context, my favourite time in flow is when I am facilitating workshops to help people extend their leadership impact and solve complex problems. For me, there is nothing better than being able to observe dynamics and throw in activities and discussion that trigger 'ah-ha' moments for people. Likewise, I am in flow when coaching people one on one to understand and act on their mental health, increase awareness of and extend their leadership impact and build team performance. Recognising what is 'flow' for you and weaving it into your working week helps develop your mental health.

Here are a few tips for maintaining and restoring your psychological energy.
1. List the different things you can do to recharge your batteries, recognising whether you are introverted, extroverted

or somewhere in between. Give yourself a few options from ones that take more planning—such as a weekend away—to ones that you can easily access when you need them such as cooking up a storm, escaping into a book, going out with close friends, enjoying a good glass of red while listening to your favourite music etc. My fail-safe way of a quick recharge is to check in with my MOMs (Meeting of the Minds group), which is my younger sister and an older brother. Being the last three of nine children, we have a very close bond. We understand each other well; we have similar approaches to work, are good at challenging each other directly and make each other laugh. We have each other's backs and can be vulnerable with each other. If I become aware that cortisol has flooded in, I like to take a walk and ring one of them to get a different perspective.

2. Once you have a list, do not wait for your energy to seriously flag before you do these activities. Build them into your habits.

3. Next, what gets you into flow? Keep a journal on this over a month or two and reflect on when you were so absorbed in loving what you were doing that nothing else mattered and you almost lost track of time. That is a good indicator of things that get you into flow. Importantly look for activities in work as much as outside work. Again, do not wait until life is challenging to access them. Build them into your plans.

———

Build in regular perspective taking

The second mindfulness tool to build your psychological health is being able to gain perspective. Once you become better at recognising the classroom inside your head and the emotions you experience, you will be able to stop and challenge yourself to gain perspective—done through the practice of gratitude. The method of stepping back and appreciating what is right rather than your brain only seeing what is wrong and feeling under threat. Gratitude, like mindfulness, is a term that is becoming more frequently used and so you may already be familiar with it. The question is, are you practising it every day?

Gratitude helps to quiet the negativity in the classroom inside your head. It helps your brain reprocess what is happening. It enables your mind to identify that which it thought was a threat as being not so significant. It helps the brain feel safe.

Harvard Medical School research[*] confirms that gratitude helps people:
- feel more positive emotions
- relish good experiences
- improve their health
- deal with adversity
- build strong relationships.

If you put into Google, 'why is gratitude important', you will find a multitude of sources supporting the science behind this technique. So, why would you not adopt this practice?

The trick is that, like exercise, gratitude cannot be wheeled out now and again with a hope this will be enough. It needs to be a

---

[*] In Praise of Gratitude, Harvard Health Publishing, Harvard Medical School. Updated June 5, 2019 (first published November 2011).

daily practice. But it is not as daunting as you may think.

When you ask someone what they are grateful for, typically family, friends and health are at the top of the list. If you are asking yourself this every day though, those three responses start to become a bit monotonous.

Here are some alternatives:
- *What is something that went well today?* No matter how bad the day was, there is always something you can find, even if it is that you are still standing at the end of the day!
- *What is something that made me smile today?* A day without a smile is a sad day. If you haven't smiled, go and watch a stand-up comedy show or something else that brings a smile to your face.
- *Who helped me in some way today that I appreciated?* Did you thank them, to build up that connection?
- *What was something I learnt today?* Being grateful for curiosity.
- *Who did I help today?* Being grateful for your ability to contribute to others.

Writing the answers to some or all of these questions each day helps to ingrain gratitude, as does sharing a reflection on gratitude each day with someone else. Or even better, telling someone else why you are grateful for something they did. That is an oxytocin and serotonin hit at the same time.

> *Stopping and appreciating life enables your brain to reset. It stops the flow of cortisol and brings back the oxytocin of connection.*

Once you have these mindfulness tools in play, do your check-in on those lag indicators of energy, emotion, classroom and environment regularly. Connecting with yourself becomes more comfortable over time. It is easiest when it becomes a habit.

How do I build the habit?

The trick to maximising your energy and your mental health is to build good habits.

If something is a habit, you do not expend precious energy on trying to motivate yourself. You just do it.

Like cleaning your teeth—you do not even stop to think about it, you just do it before you leave the house in the morning and before you go to bed.

But this is easier said than done. To build good habits understanding your bad habits first is useful.

Charles Duhigg, who wrote *The Power of Habit*[*], explains that every one of our habitual behaviours is there because of a trigger in the environment (an antecedent) and a consequential benefit that reinforces it (see Figure Eleven).

Understanding the bad habits that get in the way of maximising your mental health helps you identify the environmental factors that set you off and the perceived benefit you are getting from this bad habit. Enabling you to seek a change in environment or a better *consequence* that can help you influence your *behaviours*.

We behave in a particular way because we 'know' that the *consequence* is a benefit. We do not always consciously know

---

[*] Duhigg, C. (2013). The Power of Habit. Why we do what we do and how to change. Random House Books. London, UK.

FIGURE ELEVEN

The ABC of Habits

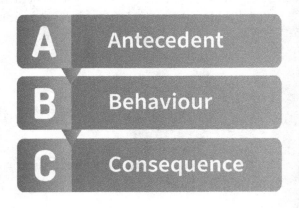

the benefit, but our mind does. I will admit I love chocolate. However, I am not always good at taking a small amount of chocolate and appreciating it. When I feel like I cannot get everything done, particularly if I have not slept enough, (*antecedent*), my brain triggers into autopilot to eat a large amount of chocolate (*behaviour*), because I know the sugar rush will make me feel better (*consequences*). Of course, it only makes me feel better for a short time, then I am back into feeling ordinary again (unless I eat more chocolate). I know that the amount of chocolate I eat is not good for me. Still, the benefits I get from the immediate hit outweigh any of the delayed concepts of feeling ordinary and ultimately putting on weight.

In recognising this as a habit and knowing that the trigger of a large volume of work in front of a computer will often be there, I aim to make it harder by three proactive actions.

1. Be disciplined in my sleep pattern, so I am more capable of dealing with the volume when it hits, decreasing the impact of the environmental trigger.

2. Change part of the environment by not having an easy to reach supply of chocolate. I know when it is in the drawer next to my desk, it is hard to resist, but if I have to go and buy it, I am more likely just to get myself a cup of my favourite tea—I keep those tea bags handy in my drawer.
3. When I cannot resist, I challenge myself to buy Lindt dark chocolate as I know I eat less of it.

Now, sure there are times when my team will attest to the fact that I am hoarding Violet Crumbles or Cadbury Roast Almond in the drawer and I fall back. I am not perfect. But I allow myself an indulgence at times then I push myself back into the proactive behaviour again.

Swapping a bad habit for a good habit builds the confidence you need to try the build the next habit then the next one. Here is a process I recommend.

1. Pick a habit that frustrates or annoys you—there is at least some willingness then to do something about it. Make sure this is clearly articulated. For example, mine is not, 'I do not eat well', it is specifically 'I overeat chocolate when I am stuck at my desk with piles of work to do, and I am tired'.
2. Pull it apart by asking questions about what events trigger the behaviour and what are the consequences (benefits). The benefits may be obvious, or you may need to dig a little deeper to identify them.
3. Can you avoid the trigger? e.g. a particular environment, person or situation?
4. Can you insert a circuit breaker where you can recognise the classroom inside your head and the emotion that comes with it and consciously then change the behaviour slightly for a better consequence? Find a consequence that is better than the current consequence.

5. Can you find a buddy? A 'Jiminy Cricket' on your shoulder pulling you back from a particular behaviour. It is why personal trainers have exploded as an industry. People want to get fit but find it hard to stay motivated, but if they have paid a personal trainer, they will not want to lose their money. The trainer pushes them.

We have a great ability to train our brains. We just need to be determined to do so.

I love the Henry Ford quote, "Whether you think you can or whether you think you can't, you are probably right." Your attitude towards what you are doing and how determined you are enables you to shift into building a different habit. Linked to this, I recommend finding a buddy who can help challenge you to get into a habit.

Once you start with one thing and it works well, document it. Remember the dopamine reaction. Your brain will love it when you set out to achieve something and achieve it. When you go back to that mental health pie, circle all the things that you already do. I have never coached a manager who has not had at least some of that pie built. So, acknowledge what you have already got in play and look at what other things in that pie you now can work on to balance it out.

———

What if I am in yellow right now?

We all go into yellow at times. Connecting to self means building the awareness that you are in yellow. Then you can ask yourself how you can bring yourself back to green. For some, this might be a long bike ride, for others spending time with friends who appreciate you or getting engrossed in your favourite hobby. (Remember that discussion in maintaining and restoring psychological energy earlier in this chapter).

If you recognise a slide into yellow and want some immediate results, there are four things I recommend:
1. Deep breathing to decrease blood pressure and bring you back into the moment.
2. Laughing to stimulate those happy chemicals.
3. Writing in a journal to reflect on what is happening and get perspective.
4. Putting earphones in with your favourite music, and if you dare sing and move to it or at least walk in the fresh air while listening.

Deep breathing

When you are in a high state of stress, often without realising, your breath tends to get shallower and faster. There is an immediate physiological benefit to consciously slowing down your breathing rate. It helps to calm the body immediately. However, to get the full benefit, I recommend practising a deep breathing exercise at the beginning of each day before you head to work. Just ten minutes a day in a quiet place. I know when I started doing deep breathing, I wondered what it achieved. However, now I can use it in the moment and feel an instant change in how I feel. Ongoing practice enables you to access that relaxed response faster when you are under stress.

Laughing

When you are feeling stressed, cortisol is thumping through your brain. Remember that as social creatures, if you feel connected, you feel safer. One of the fastest ways to trigger this is through laughter. When you laugh with someone, there is a feeling that you are both connected because of the same thing that makes you laugh. So, if deep breathing is not working as quickly as you like, bring humour into play. Call up a friend who always makes you laugh or watch an episode of your all-time favourite TV comedy or stand-up comedian. Laughter seriously is the best medicine.

Writing

Never underestimate the power of writing down your thoughts. When you find that classroom inside your head will not stop a negative loop, open up your journal and start writing. The conscious process of expressing how you are feeling on paper helps your brain process what is going on. You can then reflect on the writing with curiosity to work out what your brain is trying to tell you.

Music

Music has an almost immediate impact on the brain. Not quite as fast as laughter, but not too far off. Music triggers dopamine as our brain picks up the patterns. It can trigger oxytocin when we feel that sense of connection to the words being sung. That someone understands us. Or could just be the enjoyment of moving to a particular beat. Have some of your favourite songs lined up for the quick fix. The music that pumps you up, makes you smile, makes you want to dance or soothes you. While you are not likely to do this at work, I can recommend singing and dancing to this favourite music to get the emotions shifting into a better space.

Breathing, laughing, writing and music help to bring immediate perspective to anything that is going wrong. These pausing techniques connect you to the present moment so you can consider what your next move will be.

You need to commit to lifelong learning in this space. The more that you can connect to self, the stronger that habit becomes over time. Take that deep breath when it is hard. Laugh even harder. Use the journal to keep reflecting. Keep adding to that playlist. You will go into yellow. It is normal. You just need to build up the response muscle to stop the slide into orange and get you back to green.

How can I strengthen my quick reactions to yellow?

1. A simple app for breathing is *Kardia*. It is free for an initial trial then a one-off purchase of $1.99, so it will not break the bank. It helps you to regulate your deep breathing. You can have the sound on or off, but it enables you to set the timing of your lungs expanding and contracting so helps you to pace yourself.
2. Make sure you have got people around you that make you laugh and keep an eye on where you are at mentally. If you are not aware of the water warming up around you, they are more likely to call you on it when you don't laugh at their jokes.
3. Buy yourself that great journal for self-reflection. For those that are not used to, or do not like writing, try using voice memos and record what you are thinking as you are driving.

The critical thing is the ability to get it out of your head and onto paper or somewhere else. No one else will be reading it, so it does not matter how incoherent it is. It helps to quiet that classroom. But never underestimate the power of the actual pen and paper.
4. Use Spotify or similar online music app to create a range of playlists.

Now that you have started to look after your mental health by connecting to yourself, you may want to consider introducing the concepts in this chapter to your team. You want them to be working on their mental health as much as you are on yours. Approach this by spending some time with the team to explain to them about the colour continuum and the mental health pie. Share your own experiences and where you found it hard. Talk about some of the things that you have done to build your pie. Then get them to reflect on and assess their pie. Give them each of the exercises that you have been going through—the lag and lead indicator assessments, the activities that they might do to connect to their physical and psychological self, and the buddies that could help them along the way. Mental health is a life long journey, so keep the conversation going in the team. Make talking about mental health as comfortable as talking about physical health is.

Key things to remember

- You need to connect to yourself and learn to read your body and animal brain.
- Get into the habit of monitoring your energy levels weekly. It is normal to have low or high energy at times, but it is important to not sit at either extreme for too long, which can drag you down the continuum.
- Get into the habit of using the mental health pie assessment at least quarterly. What you focus on at any one point in time will shift, but a balanced pie is what you are after overall, where you can call on any area depending on your needs.
- Connecting to yourself and others, helping others and learning new things by remaining curious, strengthens your mental health.
- You need to build these things into a habit.
- Deep breathing, laughing, writing and music are valuable tools to get you back to green.

Use the insights from connecting to yourself to build yourself a great mental health pie and keep practising awareness of how you are moving up and down that continuum. Once you understand your pie, work on getting your teams to build their pies.

A team committed to and openly sharing their mental health journey is a powerful force for broader change as well as a powerful force for high performance.

With your team committed to their mental health, it is time to shift gears in the next chapter to building even more significant mental health and performance through how you build a direct connection with your team.

CHAPTER SIX

THE CURRENCY OF CONNECTION

When you think of the managers you have worked with throughout your career, I suspect, like mine, they fall into three distinct categories. Those you absolutely loved working for, those you struggled working for and those that sat in a neutral zone and had no real impact on you. When I reflect on my own experiences, thinking of those that I loved working with makes me smile. They understood me, they stretched my learning, and I grew as a leader because of them.

I can remember one manager from my early management days who had a very different style to me. It reached a point where I realised that before he even opened his mouth, I would be annoyed by him. It is fair to say that during that turbulent time neither he nor the team got the absolute best of me. At the heart of it was that I felt disconnected from him. This disconnection led to me struggling to connect with my team completely.

Back in Chapter Two, we talked about how connection is critical to survival. If we do not feel connected, our brains are not able to listen effectively. They cannot take in the information effectively because our patterns of thinking and the subsequent negative chemicals are overwhelming us. We are often unaware of how the brain is subconsciously working and impacting on us. Because we are pattern-seeking creatures, we need to feel connected to function effectively.

In building the 'connection with others' component of your mental health pie, you will have looked at who truly understands you. Who creates that sense of belonging and security for you? Now that you are confident looking after your mental health, it's time to look at how you connect with your team. Connection, which we know builds good mental health on a personal level, is an ever-expanding circle at work. As a manager, connecting with a team member to enable them to learn and grow, builds your mental health. Why? Because it triggers serotonin when you are helping someone else. This connection also triggers oxytocin and serotonin for the team member as they feel safe and valued. In turn, enabling you to trigger their curiosity to learn and grow—which triggers dopamine. And on it goes—the ever-expanding circle of connection.

Connection with your team is valuable currency. If you can get connection right, then you can land feedback to which the team member will listen. This will trigger curiosity, which triggers learning, which builds their confidence. Then, results here we come!

In this chapter, we will look at how to build connection to open up your ability to help others learn and grow. I'll talk about the 's**t sandwich' of feedback and why it does not work in the way that you may have learnt. I'll then introduce you to a useful and straightforward model for giving feedback. Next, you will assess your classroom inside your head, to make sure you can provide effective feedback. Then I'll flip the table and cover the value of getting feedback from your team on your shadow, which helps to build connection. This ability is all about building up your currency in the workplace. A worthwhile investment.

———

Do you see me?

Susan David[*] introduced me to the African Zulu greeting 'Sawubona'. In our Western World, the term 'How are you?' is used on automatic without even thinking about whether we want to hear the answer. Sawubona translates to 'I see you', this is what connection is—I see you. I am conscious of wanting to explain this term 'connection' without it feeling like some warm and fluffy type of comment that can tune some senior managers out. If you have read *Good to Great* by Jim Collins, you will recognise this quote:

"Those who build great companies understand that the ultimate throttle on growth for any company is not markets, or technology, or competition, or products. It is one thing above all others: the ability to get and keep enough of the right people."

For me, that is what it's all about. You get and keep enough of the right people if people feel connected to you as a leader. In 2018, Sturt and Nordstrom[†] quoted research by the O.C. TannerLearning Group[‡]

---

[*] Susan David, PhD, is a psychologist on the faculty of Harvard Medical School, cofounder and codirector of the Institute of Coaching at McLean Hospital and CEO of Evidence Based Psychology.

[†] Sturt, D and Nordstrom, T. 10 Shocking Workplace Stats you need to know. Forbes. March 8 2018.

[‡] O.C. Tanner Learning Group White Paper, Performance: Accelerated. A new benchmark for initiating employee engagement, retention and results.

based on a ten-year 200,000-person study which showed that 79% of people who quit their job cite lack of appreciation. Recognition is the number one thing employees say their managers could give them, to inspire them to do great work. We all need to feel that the work we are doing is recognised in some way—that we have been seen.

Connection, however, is much more than having a cake every month to celebrate birthdays. Although not wrong, this is not connection. You have to understand what makes people tick if you want to connect and get the best out of them. As John C. Maxwell[*] says,

"The ability to connect with others is a major determining factor in reaching your potential."

Remember, the reason is as much to help your career, as it is to help the team around you. I see managers making the mistake time and again of thinking what makes them feel valued and connected is what they then give to others. Reaching a senior level usually means you have learnt to be resilient along the way. To 'make do' to get to where you want to go. To focus on giving yourself feedback, not relying on others. But more often than not, getting to a senior level has meant you have had someone more senior to you mentoring you through. The risk of you just focusing on 'talent' at the top is you end up not getting the best performance results. You need people across your teams to feel a connection to get the best from them.

Some people are easier to connect to than others. I understand that. But we have to remember that if we only had people around us that were easy to be around, then we would not get the best decision-making within our business. We need cognitive diversity to get better outcomes. As leaders, to build the team that we want, we have to work to connect to people from all walks of life. It does

---

[*]   Maxwell, John. C.(2010). Everybody Communicates, Few connect. Harper Collins Leadership. USA.

not mean being best friends or going out for drinks regularly. It does mean that everyone in the team feels seen, feels heard, and believe that they matter. A useful starting point in building this currency of connection is to write down what you believe you know about each of your team.

Begin with a basic profile:
- How long have they lived in this location?
- Do they have family or close friends here?
- Do they have a partner?
- Do they have kids?
- Do they have pets?
- Have they got elderly parents that they're looking after?
- What are they passionate about outside work?
- What are the challenges that they face in life?
- What do you think motivates them?

When you have done that, think about what the common link between you and the other person is. Is it having kids? Enjoying the same books? Exercise? Whatever it is, that is the starting point for building a sense of connection with that person. See them as who they are. Find common ground.

I have seen managers who would prefer to just get on with the task at hand every day. They perceive a risk that they could end up spending the whole day 'connecting' and not 'doing'. For the inexperienced manager, that is absolutely a risk. Leadership is always a juggling act. You juggle the task you have to deliver on, the team dynamics and the individuals in the team—along with looking after yourself as an individual. It is a juggle, but putting down the ball that is connecting to individuals is not an option if you want long term results. I never said leadership was easy. But it is worth it.

FIGURE TWELVE

Juggling what it takes to be a leader

Does the s**t sandwich really work?

If you've been in leadership roles for a while, you've likely been introduced to the s**t sandwich of feedback. Remember the one? You start with something positive, then the negative, and finish off with positive feedback. It's built on the premise of ratios—for every negative criticism that you are going to give; you should provide somewhere between four and seven positive pieces of feedback.

But does it work?

As is often the case, we humans want the easy answer and mathematically apply this, with managers focused either on counting up the pieces of positive feedback or trying to create them from thin air to give the negative feedback they want to give. But is this effective?

Let's go back to the science of mental health to understand what 'positive' feedback can and should be.

I talked earlier about the manager that drove me nuts. I still experience that with different people in a work context. If I am expecting criticism because that is what I tend to get from them, then the cortisol is already running in my head, and it is hard to listen effectively. It takes an effort to flip into the right frame to be able to understand the valuable information underneath how it is delivered. That is the case for your teams. If a manager is only criticising them, or their positive feedback is not recognising them for who they are, they're not going to listen to it in a way that brings out their best. Their brains are processing the criticism as a threat triggering cortisol. They need the oxytocin and serotonin to balance it out.

We all need to feel safe and have that oxytocin activated. We all need to be valued and have that serotonin triggered. If you can reshape your thinking around 'positive' feedback to be a way of saying 'Sawubona'—I see you—this should automatically make 'feedback' a little easier. We will all make mistakes. Your team members need to be able to take feedback when they have not performed. But when you find them getting defensive in response to this feedback, stop and reflect. How well do you know this person? How often have you passed the time of day with them? Talked about your common ground? How often do you show appreciation for what they are doing?

Ultimately, if they feel seen, heard, and that they matter, they will take on that criticism and change because far less cortisol is triggered. Indeed, when you build this connection to the next level, they will see your 'opportunity for improvement' as you are seeing them also—that you care enough to help them learn and this will trigger their serotonin and dopamine. But if they do not first feel safe and valued for who they are, they cannot see the negative feedback as a learning opportunity. So, ditch the s**t sandwich. Do not force yourself to find a way of 'cushioning' the

PRACTICAL STEPS:

The habit of recognition

Each Friday, in your diary or your electronic calendar, post a reminder asking, 'Who have you recognised this week?' Give it a specific time slot. Ask yourself whether you have spent enough time this week recognising people. Who else do you need to consciously go out and thank for things that they had done over this week to keep building up the currency of connection?

feedback. Start with understanding your team and find common ground. Find opportunities to show your team they are valued. When criticism is needed, you are then able to do that because you've built up your currency along the way. You do not then need to 'create' positive feedback to coach them.

We can fall into the trap of looking up and reflecting down too much. If you are looking to your manager and do not feel valued, but rather feel pressure and criticism, the risk is that you'll reflect that same behaviour. You know how ordinary it feels. You know how it lands with you when you do not get the appreciation you believe you deserve.

> *You cannot change the way your manager gives you feedback, but you can and should own your shadow.*

It's a cliché to say treat others the way you want to be treated, but it is still a good motto. I appreciate it is not always easy to provide feedback, even when you have started to build connection. So read on, for ways to build your feedback muscle, to create the connection currency in your bank.

133

Is there a better way to give feedback that counts?

What do you think your immediate reaction might be to someone who says to you, 'You were rude in that meeting,' or 'You did not value my opinion in that meeting'? They are confronting statements to hear. If you are human, you are likely to feel defensive, even if you have a connection building with this other person. Having built up a connection from understanding and valuing the person, you have opened the door to be able to give feedback on where they aren't hitting the mark. If the feedback content or delivery is poor however, it will not be effective in influencing change.

So, let me change your life like mine was changed. I want to introduce you to the situation, behaviour, impact—SBI-feedback model. My thanks to the Centre for Creative Leadership for creating this model*.

I used to think I wasn't good at receiving criticism. Then a manager gave me a brilliant piece of criticism. It was clear, it was direct, it came from a clear desire to extend me, and I could learn from it. I felt valued by this manager because he was prepared to be direct with me. I realised that it was not criticism per se that I was not good at receiving, but *the way it was delivered,* which often caused a cortisol trigger. When I discovered the SBI model, I realised that was the way that particular manager gave feedback. When giving feedback using this model, it is much easier to respond rather than react and shut down. The great news is that it works just as well for giving positive feedback. Using this model for both forms of feedback enables people to learn.

As you will have guessed from the name, there are three specific things to think about in the SBI feedback model. Let's work through them.

---

* www.ccl.org – a global provider of executive education

Situation

It's essential to give a specific time and location when providing feedback to someone. It's not useful to say, 'You usually...' or, 'You always...' or, 'You often...' It does not give any context, and our brains need context to process the information quickly. Ideally, the situation is recent. Feedback on something that happened years or even months ago is not useful as it takes effort for the other person to cast their mind back. It is much better to start with, 'In the meeting this morning...' or, 'Yesterday when we were discussing...'—The specific place and time enable a clear contextual focus.

Behaviour

Give specific, observable actions rather than assumptions of what you think is going on with that person's emotions. Remember, you do not know what is going on in the classroom in their head. The only thing you can do is comment on behaviour. You cannot say 'You are angry', 'You are stressed', or 'You are upset' because they may be feeling a different emotion and labelling it differently. When you label their emotion, they can get defensive. But you can say, 'You raised your voice', 'You were frowning', 'you did not say anything' or whatever is an observable *behaviour*, not an emotion.

Impact

The impact is about the effect on you. Essentially, you are telling this person what happened in the classroom inside your head and how you felt about that person's words or actions. Thus, the connection starts because you are prepared to be open about your feelings to help the person pause and think about their actions. It is the difference between saying 'you were rude' which can trigger a defensive cortisol fuelled reaction and 'I felt like you did not value my opinion. I am pretty sure you did not mean to do that, but that is how I felt'.

Look at the difference between just saying, 'Great job on that call yesterday,' and 'Yesterday, you took a tough call (*Situation*), and you kept your voice at an even level. You paused so that that customer who was yelling could say what they needed to say, and you managed to get through the entire conversation without raising your voice once at them (*Behaviour*). I am so impressed that you were able to do this. I think you could teach me a thing or two' (*Impact*). The second way builds currency. The first way is fleeting and does not cue the person into what was so great and how significant it was to you.

When you are giving negative feedback, you use the same model, but at the end of the SBI, you would say, 'Help me to understand'. For example, if you say, 'In the meeting yesterday, we were talking about XYZ. When I questioned what you were doing (*Situation*), you raised your voice (*Behaviour*). I was worried about you, as this is not a typical response (*Impact*). Help me understand what is going on for you right now'. This feedback and question, rather than just 'Are you okay after that meeting?' is a more powerful and faster way to build the currency of connection.

The SBI model helps to set out the rhythm of the feedback. It's less threatening and makes the person feel more connected. I can think of countless examples of how this has worked well in the coaching space. But I want to talk about two specific examples that stand out to me.

I often facilitate workshops on enabling great feedback within teams. Where appropriate, I take these teams through an exercise that can be an uncomfortable situation for some. If I believe a leader is ready, I get their team to give feedback to them in front of me. Enabling the team to provide feedback in a safe environment where we can work on finessing the message. Here are two powerful pieces of feedback that were insightful and had a profound positive impact on the managers.

One person said, 'You know that I am going through a difficult relationship breakdown. Yesterday when we had our one-to-one meeting (*Situation*), you happened to notice that my wedding ring was missing. You asked me if I wanted to talk about it and I said no. And we went on with the rest of the conversation (*Behaviour*). But you have no idea how much that meant to me, that you would notice something as small as that and be willing and wanting to talk about it. You grabbed my loyalty and respect in that moment. And I just wanted to say thank you.' Wow. A side-comment. No further conversation. But that currency of connection was built. And the person prepared to tell their manager of the impact built that currency of connection even further.

Likewise, I had a manager that said to his manager, 'Three weeks ago, you were on my site walking around (*Situation*). I had been working extensively on XYZ before your visit because of prior questions you had asked. Yet, in the conversation you didn't ask any questions on this and instead moved quickly to other topics (*Behaviour*). I felt a real sense of resentment and frustration given how much time I had spent working on this issue in my own time (*Impact*). And I am pretty sure you did not mean to make me feel resentful and frustrated, but that is how I felt.' This was a great example of disconnection, but also a way of building connection when the team member was prepared to say this. The manager had no recollection of this particular conversation and no awareness of how long this person had spent on the issue prior. They had thought the site visit had gone well. This feedback gave the manager a view of the shadow he cast without realising, but also strengthened the relationship between the two of them—the willingness of both of them to give and receive this honest feedback built connection.

It can feel clunky and fake when you first start. And it will keep feeling that way until you get into the swing of it. But this is about how you build connection as a team. It is not about always being positive; it's about building a safe and honest environment. That is where the magic lies.

I do appreciate though that it's not as easy as it looks. There are a few common mistakes that people make.

The first one is being non-specific about the situation. If you generalise multiple events, people's brains cannot process as well. Or if the situation has long since passed, the other person may have no memory of what happened.

The second one is around behaviour that cannot be observed. If you jump into, 'You were rude', or 'You were angry' it is easy for the other person to become defensive. But they cannot argue with observations such as, 'You raised your voice'. Make sure that you are specific on behaviour that anyone walking past could also see. There is no judgement or interpretation of behaviour; it is just stated behaviour.

The third is around how *you* felt. That is the part that builds a connection with the other person. What is the impact on you, as a leader? 'I thought it was great', is not powerful, nor is 'the team feel...'. But saying; 'I am proud', 'I am relieved', or 'I am confident because of the way you were doing things', are the emotions that the other person needs to hear. It is through understanding our emotional impact on others that we can learn how to understand and connect with the other person. This is going to make the difference and builds currency.

Three tips while you are learning this technique:
• Write it down and make sure you have each element: situation, behaviour, impact.
• Test it on someone else, in the beginning.
• Reflect afterwards about what worked or did not work.

It is just like training for a marathon. The first day, you are not going to be able to run a marathon. You've got to build up the strength for it. Just accept that it's going to be a little clunky until you get used to it and enjoy the learning process. Remember that weekly reminder in your diary or calendar from above? Use the SBI model each time you give feedback each week. That is the best way to strengthen the muscle.

Is there a right and wrong time to give feedback?

The answer is yes. The risk with feedback is that we can jump in and give feedback when it does not help the other person.

Before you start to give feedback, ask yourself these questions:
- What is going on for me right now?
- What is going on in the classroom inside my head?
- Are my emotions stable enough to give this feedback?

The ultimate question, however, is why am I giving this feedback? Am I giving this feedback to connect and help the other person, or is it just to get anger, frustration or annoyance off my chest?— They are two very different reasons. The risk in getting it off your chest is what I call faulty serotonin. Serotonin kicks in when we feel a sense of strength—a strength of rightness if you like. If you want to give this feedback because you believe you are right and they are wrong, do not. You always want to provide feedback to someone in the context of helping them and building a connection. Not to make yourself feel better.

If you are comfortable there is value in giving the feedback, the next questions are about the other person:
- What is going on for them right now?
- Do you think that they are going to be in the right space to hear this?

You are not going to know what is going on in the classroom inside their head. However, if it is clear the person is still agitated about the situation, or you know there are still external factors in the environment impacting them, then it's not useful to give them feedback right at that time. Express concern and care yes, but give feedback on where they could improve, no. Let them get perspective first.

Finally, there are questions that you need to ask yourself after providing feedback if you want to master and build the currency of connection.
- Did you stick to the SBI and nail all three?
- Did the other person respond in a way that was not defensive?
- Do you need to talk to them again on this topic, or are you confident that this team member or colleague or manager has benefited from the feedback that you have given?

The most important thing to remember is that feedback is not about being right or having the truth of a situation. Feedback is about wanting to help others, to trigger their curiosity to learn to do something differently. And to build connection. Remember, we all need to feel like we have been seen, we have been heard, and that we matter. If you can come from a perspective of truly wanting to help someone, then the feedback has the best ability to make the connection.

I had a situation where one of my team made a major mistake in some information she had sent externally, which was going to cause a few challenges for us. I needed the issue like a hole in the head, but I never gave feedback about how I felt or what she did wrong. I went calmly into solution mode. I did not express anger in my conversation with her. Later, she asked me why I did not tell her how angry and disappointed I was about her mistake as she felt she deserved my anger. I asked her, 'What would it have done to help you at that time?' She laughed and said, 'Nothing'. I said, 'You were beating yourself up enough. You knew that this was a problem, and you knew how to fix it. The most important thing I could do then was to support you. It was irrelevant to ask about how this happened. You just needed my support'. Both these interactions built a connection between us.

Another interaction sticks in my mind, given the benefit I gained from pausing and challenging myself about why I reacted the way I did. During a meeting, a colleague criticised me in front of everyone else for putting the numbers before the people. I was quite angry at the criticism given my passion for engaging people and my view of this being a convenient deflection by him. I remained calm in the meeting, but the interaction bothered me. Because of my commitment to building connection through feedback, I wanted to give him feedback so that he could understand the true impact of his behaviour. In the first instance, I thought he could learn from understanding this impact. But I chose to pause because I appreciated that I was angry. I needed to get rid of that anger before I decided if giving feedback was helping him, or just getting something off my chest.

By stopping and thinking about it, I was able to listen to what I believed he was saying underneath it and what I could learn from it. In the end, I did give him the feedback through the SBI model but gave him a thank you card at the same time given what I had learnt. I said to him, 'In that meeting last week (*Situation*), you said that I wasn't approaching the issue in the right way (*Behaviour*). I felt really angry (*Impact*), and I'm pretty sure that you did not mean to make me feel angry. But I also want to thank you. Even though I did not like hearing that message, when I stopped and thought about it, I know the reason I was angry was that there was a kernel of truth in what you said. It has made me challenge myself about what else I can do in my communication. (A second more positive *Impact*). So, thank you!'

The pause allowed me to realise there was learning for me in there. I did not think the way the criticism was delivered was appropriate, but I could learn from it. It was also valuable to give him feedback about his unintended impact on me. I think I could have knocked him over with a feather when I handed him the thank you card. He immediately confirmed he had no intention of making me angry and was sorry he did but also loved the acknowledgement of the card. It built a much better connection of trust between us because of this honest conversation. That is what the currency of connection is all about.

You may think it is valuable that your team—or others—know when you are angry or frustrated or disappointed with them because they know they need to do better. But the intensity of those emotions can trigger a strong cortisol reaction in others. I love Eckhart Tolle's saying, 'You are never upset for the reason you think'. Stop and reflect. Why are you feeling angry, frustrated or upset? What else is going on for you? In the situation above, my instant reaction was anger because he was confrontational. But with time to reflect, I could recognise if I were completely comfortable with how I was approaching the situation, I would have been able to respond to the situation calmly. The reflection enabled me to understand my frustrations with what was, and was not, working in my telling of the story.

Yes, the team need to know when they have not met the mark. Yes, it is valuable for them to understand your feelings. But you have to remember that they did not set out to make you feel angry or frustrated or annoyed. They are trying to do the best they can with what they have got. Ask yourself, 'What is the most important thing I can do to help this team member right now?'

The golden rules to stick by:
- Do not give feedback when your emotions are running high.
- Always come from a perspective of connecting to help them be a better version of themselves/solve a problem, not of you being right.

Write out the SBI model, carry it in your diary, and ask the pre- and post-feedback questions above, to keep building the feedback muscle.

It may not always work, despite your best efforts, because it depends on the classroom inside the other person's head. But when it does work, it lands brilliantly. Remember that feeling, because that is what will keep you going with it. And when someone responds poorly given their classroom, see it as an opportunity to learn more about what makes them tick.

———

How can I keep learning and growing?

To build a connection to its fullest, this SBI feedback needs to be able to go both ways. If you are willing to take on feedback, your team are going to be more accepting of your feedback. This enables you to get them into the mentally healthy high-performance space. We all have unexpected ways in which we have an impact on others. If you do not get feedback on your impact, you will not be able to learn where your intent does not match the impact.

PRACTICAL STEPS:

Building team confidence in giving you feedback on your impact

I get that it's daunting. The challenge is that you might feel like you have opened up a floodgate and the team will think, 'Great. I can give my boss all sorts of feedback.' That is not valuable.

The best way to start this is to acknowledge things about your behaviour that you want to improve. For example, if I wanted to acknowledge my tendency to interrupt people, I could tell a team member or two before meetings,' I am focusing on not interrupting people when they are talking. I want you to give me feedback at the end. Use the SBI model.' That is the best way for people to start feeling comfortable because you are acknowledging this is a weakness for you and asking for SBI feedback around this specific meeting. It also role models to them how they can seek input on their blind spots.

The value of this feedback model is the ability for both parties to get insights into each other to build connection. I encourage you to stop and listen to each piece of feedback given. I sometimes find it is valuable to write down the feedback that someone has given you to then reflect on it. Regardless of your intent, what you do does impact others in different ways. The feedback they give you about your shadow gives you a window into the classroom inside their head. That is how you connect.

One of the biggest 'ah-ha!' moments for me, was when I introduced the SBI model to a national team I was leading several years ago. I had encouraged them in their practice of the model to feel comfortable giving the feedback up, down or sideways. One of my direct reports chose to give that feedback to me. He said, 'Genevieve, can you remember the meeting last week when we were trying to solve problem X? When we were trying to solve it, I was giving some ideas on how we could fix it (*Situation*), and you cut across me to put your ideas forward about how we would solve it (*Behaviour*). It made me feel like you did not value my opinion' (*Impact*).

Here is the fascinating thing about that feedback. I could remember the meeting, but what I remembered was that I was excited about the idea generation. In my brainstorming, I was oblivious to the fact that I had cut someone else off. I valued this team member's feedback, but this was a classic intent not matching impact. I had cast a shadow unintentionally. I was completely oblivious. My response to this person was to apologise. I said 'I am really sorry. I have no recollection of the fact that I interrupted you in that way. And I want to be clear—I value your opinion. I am sorry that you felt that way and I'll make sure that I am aware of that in the way in which we interact in the future. Can I also say thank you for letting me know? I really appreciate it.'

If he had instead chosen to say, 'Genevieve, in the meeting last week, you did not value my opinion,' you can imagine that I would have been immediately defensive. It would not have made sense to me because I knew I did value his opinion. Because he was able to use the SBI model, I got a big 'ah-ha!' moment from a completely unintended impact.

This particular piece of feedback was building currency of connection in several ways.

1. Our relationship strengthened. From the way I responded, he felt more comfortable to give me feedback again if needed, and I trusted him to be completely honest in this feedback.
2. I got a good insight into what I could specifically do to make sure he felt valued.

3. His leadership strengthened. From the way I responded, he could see the value of the SBI feedback and therefore was more confident using this model with others.
4. I realised that I do interrupt others during idea generation. I might blame it on being one of nine children—if you wanted to be heard you often had to interrupt others! As a family, that is the way we rolled, and I thought nothing of it. What I had not appreciated is how that could make someone else feel.

Your ability to show your vulnerability in taking on feedback from the team builds connection leading to trust between you skyrocketing, and the ability to solve problems together increases. Both build good mental health for everyone in the team. So why would you not want to encourage this feedback?

———

Key things to remember

Connection is critical.
- It is essential to connect with your team to start giving feedback.
- You need to start with understanding who they are and what your common ground is. When you can converse on a social level, on a common interest, this helps to relax people.
- Feedback should only be given from a position of helping to build connection and learning. Not to vent, or air grievances, with your team.
- The Situation, Behaviour, Impact model is a simple but effective tool to diffuse tension in giving feedback.

Any time you want to give feedback, you need to ask yourself:
- Am I in an emotionally stable place to provide the feedback?
- Do I believe the other person is in an emotionally stable place to receive feedback?
- Am I giving the feedback to build connection and help rather than to be right?

So, from here, actively start to get to know your team. Use the SBI model to give recognition, again and again, to build confidence within the team. Also, use the SBI model to provide constructive feedback that triggers curiosity in them to learn. You should then start coaching the team on the SBI model. Do not underestimate how powerful this is. Your ability to recognise and appreciate each other, to have honest conversations when things are not working well, to have vulnerable conversations when you are struggling, to have direct and open conversations when you see someone else struggling, builds the sort of connection that forms a high-performing team with good mental health. That is the currency of connection.

I know you do not operate in a vacuum in an organisation. In the next chapter, we are going to look at how you can get your team mentally healthy and high performing, by pulling apart the issues getting in the way of their performance in the organisation and helping them get back into the driver's seat of their results.

CHAPTER SEVEN

FROM CONNECTION TO CURIOSITY TO CONTROL – THE MAGIC FORMULA

'I am just a little cog in a big machine, what can I do?' is a familiar comment from people working in medium to large organisations. What can you honestly do to change the 'way things are done around here'? But here is a question to ponder: where would we be if we did not have those who believed change is possible? I challenge you to imagine an organisation, let alone a world, without people who believed systems could change. I am not suggesting protests and sit-ins here, rather a mindset shift in the way you and your team think about problems in the workplace.

You now know curiosity is one of the critical ingredients that feeds your mental health. Now you need to shift that way of thinking to the broader landscape of team curiosity. This chapter is about how you trigger curiosity, again and again, to get your team back into the driver's seat of control.

Feeling in control is a crucial component of mental health. It decreases cortisol and builds serotonin through confidence.

It's the combination of individual mental health and the team's collective commitment to creating a mentally healthy working environment that delivers the best results personally and professionally. Curiosity is a non-negotiable ingredient in this mix. You can create the best of relationships, the best of connections with the team. You can feel like you understand each other, but connection will only get you so far if the team feels like they are drowning, that their choices are being made by the rest of the organisation. Negativity will creep in.

Strong connection in the team in a difficult environment results in vulnerability to negativity unless you can trigger curiosity.

Once a team is connected, you have the best chance of them being open to curiosity—a 'what if' and 'why not' state of mind. Triggering curiosity is about asking yourself and your team different questions that get the team exploring this 'what if' and 'why not' arena.

Curiosity changes the mindset from a sense of fear and frustration, to a desire to explore what can change within the environment to improve the current situation.

Curiosity in and of itself does not give control. Curiosity is the mindset that helps us ask different questions and rethink the threat as an opportunity that we can solve—Triggering dopamine as we start to work out new patterns and serotonin when we build confidence in our ability to control 'threats'. Doing it together produces oxytocin. This combination is what builds good mental health as a team.

Daniel Siegel, the author of *Mindsight*[*], notes, "when we block our awareness of feelings, they continue to affect us anyway. Research has shown repeatedly that even without conscious awareness, neural input from the internal world of our body and emotion influences our reasoning and our decision making." This input is amplified in a team environment. Negative emotions within a team can drag a whole team into the yellow, if not some into orange. On the flip side, collective curiosity triggers a team back to green. It enables the team to ask, 'what is triggering this emotion for us all?', 'what can we do differently here to not get frustrated, demotivated or annoyed?'

Faulty reasoning and decision making are not helpful to your team. You need your team to flip from feeling they are 'not in the driver's seat' to becoming curious about what they can change— From powerless little cog in a big machine to owners of their destiny. If you get your team triggered into a collective sense of curiosity, then you get two for the price of one. You solve some of the problems that you face as a team within an organisation *and* build collective mental health. The organisation and the individual both win through this process.

In this chapter, you are going to learn about a team-based methodology I have been using for more than 15 years. A process focused on collective mental health through team-based problem-solving, which is a crucial skillset for any team to learn. It's not about a specific problem. It's about applying an approach that keeps the team in a state of curiosity each time a problem comes up. I will take you through the methodology, then get you to reflect on how you hold the team to account for the ongoing actions. We will also explore the role you play as a leader in

* Siegel, Daniel, J. MD (2012). Mindsight: Change your brain and your life. Scribe Publications Pty Ltd. London, UK.

continuing to trigger curiosity and connection through storytelling—The biggest connector of all time.

———

Are you curious enough to trigger curiosity in others?

Curiosity is food for the brain. Your challenge is to understand whether you are in a curious state of mind yourself—another case of needing to put your oxygen mask on first. You cannot help others unless you can put the techniques into practice yourself.

During the global financial crisis, I was working in what can only be described as a mentally unhealthy workplace. The tension between the various teams was high. The 'blame game' was occurring, poor behaviour was being left unchecked, and I was feeling stuck. My business partner and I had sold our business to this organisation, and I was contracted to stay for two years or lose the cash payment of the sale. I was stuck in this record loop of thinking, 'This is a horrible environment, but I have got to put up with it to get my golden handshake.' My husband could see the effect it was having on me. He challenged me to leave the organisation. In his words, 'The money is not worth the effect on your health'. I was at a crossroads, and I agreed with my husband. The money wasn't worth losing my health. I took a break to reflect. Being the stubborn and determined person that I am, I did not want this environment to defeat me, but I had to change to defeat it.

I started with recalibrating my priorities to get enough sleep, healthy food, adequate exercise. Easier said than done, but I had to begin with this oxygen mask. I was able to recognise I could not do it on my own. All the hours of work had left me not connecting with people that could help. So, I reconnected with people who I knew could support and challenge me to look after my health. Then my thinking went deeper—I knew that I couldn't change anything, nor support my team if I remained with this feeling of being stuck. I needed to put into practice what I preached. I needed to either get curious or leave. The choice was mine. I recognised deep within me my strong determination to make a difference. I reflected that I might face this dynamic anywhere—I could move to another organisation and still find these poisonous politics (sadly they exist everywhere).

So, I flipped my mindset to curiosity. I asked myself:
- What do I need to learn from this situation?
- What could this environment teach me, that could help me for future environments?
- How can I help others in this environment to look after themselves too?

It was a significant shift for me. The number of qualifications I have is a good indicator of my love of learning. I know I am at my best when I can both teach and learn. So, I shifted my mindset to 'this is a learning opportunity'. I started each day with that curious question, 'I wonder what I will learn today?'. At the end of each day, I wrote a note in my diary on what I learnt. It was mostly about myself—what was triggering a response in me. But it was also what I learnt about others—what I tried in order to trigger a different reaction. It was about what worked and did not work, and my insights into why I thought some things worked and others did not.

It wasn't an overnight change. But my belief in staying curious to learn kept me going. I learnt so much about myself in that time. I grew stronger as a leader. In fact, when the two years clicked over, I could take my golden handshake—instead, I remained for a further four years! I did not recognise at the time how much cortisol was constantly flooding through me. It was affecting my reasoning and decision making. I was nowhere near performing the way I was capable, and I needed to make a change consciously. My curious mindset triggered learning. In turn, it was triggering dopamine that kept me in a curious state. It did not change the environment, but I could see what I was learning. I can now look back on that time and smile at how much I have learned from that. Certain things do not bother me now because of the skills that I learned then. But I needed that shift to be curious to get out of a negative mindset.

If you are feeling stuck in your organisation, then you cannot be effective at helping others.

Before you embark on this next phase of facilitating curiosity, take a long hard look at yourself.
- Do you believe despite being only part of the machine, that you can influence the machine?
- Do you believe there are ways of working within the team that can change?
- Check-in on that classroom inside your head. How often are the same negative loops coming up about work?

In my story, I was the frog in the water that was rapidly warming up. I was in the orange and at risk of sliding into the red. I was lucky enough to have my husband looking out for me. I was able to reflect then and make a call on the 'stay or go'. In this case, I chose to stay but only because I could flip to a curious state. I am glad I did, as I am stronger for what I learnt. However, it was borderline there for a while with me sitting in orange. If you are trying to stay curious, but you are showing symptoms of being stuck in orange or even sliding toward red, then you need to make a call when curiosity is not enough in this environment, and you need to get out. This decision is not a failure in any way; it is you recognising the environments that are conducive or not to your mental health. This is a wise and strong decision. You can then use this change to reflect on what you have learnt from your experiences that you will apply in a healthier situation. Either way, you focus on triggering curiosity to build mental health.

———

How can I stay curious?

Two great questions to stay curious. One for self-reflection and one for conversation:
- What can I learn from this situation?
- Can you help me understand?

Anytime that you are feeling a sense of annoyance or frustration bubbling up, there is something there for you to learn. The classroom inside your head has been triggered in some way. So, take a deep breath and ask yourself whether this is a time for self-reflection or conversation.

If it is a self-reflection moment, then write down the situation, then write down the question, 'What can I learn from this?'. Sometimes the learning is evident. Sometimes it might take going for a run or doing something else physical to distract your mind, then coming back to the question.

If it is a time for a conversation—the annoying feeling is just not going away, use the SBI model to explore that with the other person. It might sound like this: 'Yesterday at the meeting (*Situation*) when you said X (*Behaviour*) I found myself feeling frustrated. (*Impact*) I am pretty sure you do not mean to make me feel frustrated, so can you help me understand your perspective and how we work more effectively together.' The critical point is to ask the other person to help you understand their perspective. It takes defensiveness off the table and opens up curiosity.

When people are stuck, they will not be as productive as they need to be. They can still get work done, but the level of energy they expend on negative thinking is not where you want them to channel their energy. In our ideal world, we want everyone in the team to get into their own driver's seat and crack on with getting the work done. And if your team is doing that right now, fantastic. But I have never seen a team that has not got stuck at some point. They may not verbalise it as feeling stuck, but you start to see excuses surface. Then comes negativity. Are you curious enough? You are curious enough if you do not have constant negative loops going in your head and when a negative loop appears, you recognise it and ask yourself a question to break the spiral of thinking and move forward.

You need to be mindful of staying in a curious state yourself, enabling you to trigger collective curiosity to understand what is getting in the way of delivering. So as long as you are convinced you can easily step into a curious mindset, then read on to how you trigger team-based curiosity to build mental health and solve problems. What a magic combination!

———

How do I build team-based curiosity?

Curiosity in a team-based environment is mental health on steroids. When we are in a curious state, we are open to learning. Our brains love learning. Remember we are pattern-seeking creatures. Learning is an 'ah-ha' moment for the brain. It gets excited as it has identified a pattern, dopamine is triggered, and curiosity builds further curiosity. The more we stay curious, the more capacity we have to keep learning. Curiosity strengthens our brain. It creates strong neural pathways which help keep our brain healthy. Siegel[*] notes "novelty, or exposing ourselves to new ideas and experiences, promotes the growth of new connections among existing neurons and seems to stimulate the growth of myelin, the fatty sheath that speeds nerve transmissions. Novelty can even stimulate the growth of new neurons." This is food for the brain that keeps us mentally healthy.

When the team solves a problem because of this curiosity, you then have collective serotonin—we are good, we achieved -and oxytocin—we achieved as a team. What a magical combination!

As a start to building team-based curiosity, introduce the team to those same two key questions:
• What can I learn from this situation?
• Can you help me understand?

On the simple issues in the workplace, these two questions work well. When you see a team member feeling frustrated or negative, perhaps cynical about a situation, challenge them to get curious and select one of those questions to answer.

There are times that you will recognise this is not about one person's frustrations, but 'group think'. The team are stuck collectively in a negative loop. The oxytocin of connection has created a 'them' and 'us' mentality, which is not helping performance. This situation is where a team-based approach needs to be implemented.

I worked with a group who were frustrated because they had high turnover and were having trouble attracting people into the

---

[*] Siegel, Daniel, J. MD (2012). Mindsight: Change your brain and your life. Scribe Publications Pty Ltd. London, UK.

team. They felt that no one wanted to join them, and therefore they could not do what they needed to because they did not have the right resources. Through the process of triggering curiosity, I got them thinking 'What is it that makes our team less attractive? What can we change? What can we do differently?' I had empathy for their frustration, but as I pointed out, it's all well and good to sit there and be negative, but their negativity was not helping to attract talent to their team. In fact, it was making it worse.

I asked them to flip it to something that they could change. The challenge for the team was 'How do we change our reputation with the rest of the organisation, so people want to work with us?'. We started with them asking themselves honestly, 'Do we want to work here ourselves?' That was their 'ah-ha' moment; they real- ised they were in a self-fulfilling prophecy. They were stuck in a negative loop and therefore, not creating the environment in which they wanted to work. So, the first step in the process was to rebuild pride in the team. The question for them to answer was, 'Even without resources, how can we create a sense of belong- ing and achievement (no matter how small) that triggers pride?' The next question was, 'How do we deliberately get out there and promote this team to change perception?'

It took about nine months of hard work and determination to get to the point where people were putting their hands up to come and join them. They built skills along the way in creating the right environment. They were also smart about how they promoted it, so people were saying, 'That is the team that I want to be part of.' What a great turnaround!

- They started with everyone stuck in negativity and feeling stressed about the vacancies in the team.
- They triggered curiosity and stayed curious.
- They halved turnover, people *wanted* to join their team, and they consistently delivered with an almost full team.

The team environment was dynamic—they could see how they could make a difference. They understood they were part of the problem, but could change themselves. In the process, their collective mental health improved as did their performance. What is not to love?

In commencing work with a team, a common challenge is, 'I cannot change what other parts of the organisation do, and what they're doing impacts me.' You are right. You cannot change other people. You cannot change other parts of the organisation. But you can change your team's perspective on the problem, and that is what we are trying to do. If you and your team become caught in the negativity loop, it is not good for your mental health, and it is not good for performance. You need to trigger the curious mindset. You never know what the problem or solution might be, but the point is that you and your team are working on it collectively and maintaining curiosity. Curiosity keeps you and the team in green.

You are mentally healthy with curiosity. You are going to perform better with curiosity.

When is the team ready for this?

In introducing the methodology to you here, I am making several assumptions. These are 'do not pass go' assumptions. In other words, this methodology will not work unless you have already taken these steps:
1. You have invested first in understanding your mental health.
2. You have built a sustainable mental health pie for yourself.

3. You have worked with the team for them to understand their mental health.
4. They have invested in building their mental health pie.
5. You are convinced, despite the challenges of the workplace, that you are in a curious mindset right now.
6. You have started to build the muscle of curiosity in the team through the use of 'What can I learn?' and 'Can you help me understand?' and they are using the SBI model for feedback.
7. You are prepared for and open to feedback you might not like about your own shadow and willing to make changes.

If you haven't taken these steps, my advice is to go back and work on these first. You will not get the benefits of this methodology unless you have put these other factors into place.

So, if you have these in place and you see your team stuck in a negative loop, then it is time to kick off with the team-based approach. Figure Thirteen gives you a simple framework for this methodology.

———

FIGURE THIRTEEN

The team-based assessment of a mentally healthy workplace.

All issues
Brainstorm what is happening in team
using the mental health checklist

One issue
Vote on the most pressing issues that the
team want to work on

Three actions
Do not overload. Don't be too ambitious. Three clear
measurable actions that can shift things.

Three months

Resolved?
Select the next issue
from the list

Not resolved?
Modify actions
and repeat

First session: getting it all out to end up with one focus area

The starting point is to sit down as a team to identify all the issues and get them on the whiteboard.
- Give a copy of the checklist below to each team member.
- Get each team member to reflect and circle the statements they answer 'no' to.
- Form small groups of 3–4 people to review answers and identify the ones that they have in common. (The individual experience needs to be faced at a personal level. It is the common experience that is best to solve collectively.)
- Each small group then writes up their top four or five issues on butchers' paper and sticks it on the wall. (There is value for the brain, in writing down rather than typing despite butchers' paper being old fashioned.)
- Everyone can read the small group lists to then consolidate into one new list so that no issues are repeated.
- Allow time for the team to read and reflect on this list quietly then give the team four stickers each to vote for problems that are bothering them the most. They can choose to put all their stickers against one problem or assign them across several problems.

This exercise starts to sort out what is the biggest issue for the team. It's not saying that the other things aren't big issues, but it's identifying what the team feels passionately about as the most negative thing. 'The tribe has spoken'. The team can sit back and see what has stood out for them collectively.

Take a photo of those votes for future reference and then turn to the one with the most votes. The next step is to unpack this issue as a team. This is where the connection you have built from working on your mental health, and your curious questioning comes into play. It is only through connection and curiosity that people can be open and honest about what is going on.

The team are more likely to look at the external factors that cause their problem first. In staying curious as a leader, after you have let them vent, you can start shifting their mindset by asking, 'How do we contribute to this problem?' and 'What can we change?'

At the end of this session, you need to come out with:
• a clearly defined problem statement focused on what the team is doing that is not helpful
• a clear set of measurable, achievable actions assigned to the team to complete in the next three months.

An example of problem-solving came from a group where their frustration was their manager, and the manager above had conflicting views about what was needed to deliver growth. The team felt confused as to what they needed to do and thought that they could not then give clear direction to their teams.

Sound familiar?

Getting into curious questioning enabled them to:
• articulate what each manager was saying clearly
• identify the common ground between the two managers—they had the same goal just a slightly different opinion on how to get there
• recognise the common goal—'the what' mattered more than the 'how' to the managers above
• work from there on the 'how' they owned as a team,
• decide as a team how to give clarity to the teams below, regardless of what the managers above said, which was critical to get them to contribute.

This then translated into specific actions for each of the team to move forward.

PRACTICAL STEPS:

Use the statements below to assess how mentally healthy your team is

Connection

- We know something about each other's background.
- We have found common ground beyond direct work with each other person in the team to build a connection.
- We can laugh as a team.
- We know how to motivate each other to deliver great performance.
- We are consciously taking actions each week to motivate each other to deliver.
- When an individual has 'failed' the team or someone in the team they feel comfortable acknowledging it to the team or the individual.
- When things go wrong, we come together to solve collectively not criticise individually.
- When team members are away, we support one another to complete key work.
- Within the team, it feels safe to acknowledge when we are struggling personally or professionally.

Curiosity

- As a team, we go outside the comfort zone to learn.
- When we face a challenge, we are good at asking curious questions to work out how to solve the problem together.
- We expect and accept a level of failure as we believe it helps us ultimately find the right solution.
- We regularly discuss 'failures' as a team to work out what we can learn and do differently as a team.
- We are comfortable responding to the constant change in the workplace.
- We are consciously triggering curiosity in the team during times of change.

Contribution

- We have position descriptions for every role.
- Every role has got measurable KPIs that link to others in the team, and the organisation.
- Everyone sees each other's KPIs.
- Those KPIs reasonable to achieve with the resources we have.
- We measure these KPIs regularly and openly, so the team knows how we are performing.
- We have the capability in the team to do the job.
- We get regular encouraging and specific feedback to keep improving.
- We give regular encouraging and specific feedback to keep improving.
- We feel valued and recognised for what we contribute inside the team.
- We feel valued and recognised for what we contribute by others outside the team.
- We consciously value and recognise our team.

Follow-up sessions: building on success

There is a reason why I have suggested stating the problem statement as well as the actions. The risk once you get into action mode is that you lose sight of the problem you were solving. The team get focused on just ticking off the actions. Every three months, take the time out as a team to revisit and reset asking yourself the following questions, for as long as is needed to ensure sustainable curiosity:

- Has the problem been solved? Has the problem diminished?
- If not, did we achieve all our actions? What got in the way of achieving them?
- Were the actions not enough? Were they the wrong ones? What have we learnt? What do we need to do differently to get these actions into play?

If you agree the problem has been solved or diminished enough that you deal with it easily, then revisit the problem list from the first session. Remove the votes and just have the list in front of them. Ask first, are those problems still our biggest issues, is there anything we would add to the list?

Then go through the voting process again and find the next problem to solve. Once the team sees the benefit of curiosity, you will find that this thinking creeps into monthly or weekly meetings, and you no longer need the bigger workshop-style problem-solving. But you continuously need to look at the dynamic of the team and how they work together. If curiosity is at the forefront of conversation you are in a good position for strong mental health and performance. If criticism and negativity are at the forefront of discussion, it is time to come back to this methodology.

You may feel that there are too many problems to solve. But this is why you only tackle one problem at a time. The voting process is a valuable part of the methodology. While you cannot solve everything, tackling one thing that everyone feels passionate about, and finding a way of solving that problem can trigger the dopamine, serotonin and oxytocin to give the confidence to solve the next problem—thus changing people's mindsets. By solving one problem at a time, you are building up good mental health along the way individually and collectively.

You may be concerned that bringing problems to the surface has the potential to make the team feel even worse. It is why I am saying 'do not pass go' until you have the first seven steps in place. However, if you are particularly concerned about the state of the team and cannot wait, I would recommend bringing in an external facilitator who can help challenge mindsets and get the process turbocharged for you. They can also offer useful insights to you on the team dynamic and areas for you to focus on as a leader. But remember you are still the Musical Director leading the song.

_____

How do I engage the team in ongoing self-belief and curiosity?

All of us have probably had team days away where everyone has been excited about a change. Then when you come back, and everyone gets back to 'reality', things get forgotten. Your role as a leader is to keep this energy going. In David Pearl's words[*] "You are meaning makers". You can help your team by telling them stories because powerful stories can trigger every one of those helpful brain chemicals.

We are hardwired for stories—confirmed by the PhDs of two prominent researchers in this area, Brené Brown and Susan David. Their research confirms that ultimately, it's emotion and not data that drives us—we can get stuck in negative loops because of the stories in our classroom inside our head. This realisation can be horrifying to people who believe they are only data-driven. But even if you think you are data-driven, it is the story that triggers something inside you. It is not the data, but the meaning, or story, you attach to that data that hooks you. You cannot get away from this; we are all driven by stories.

Think about this from the perspective of politicians or the media. They know that whoever controls the narrative wins—the votes or the money depending on where you play. Politicians want to tell a story that can hook people. They use the statistics that

_____

[*] David Pearl is an innovator in Business, the Arts and Social Change and is the author of the book 'Story for Leaders' published in 2016 by London Business Forum, London.

suit them to shape their stories. Politicians see that our collective brains respond strongly to fear. They want to create fear about what the opposition will do for you to believe they are the safer option. The brain is tricked into looking for a threat, seeing the danger and triggering cortisol, then identifying a safe solution to get the oxytocin to flow again, likewise, with the media. The media do not want a story that is 'true' if it is not exciting, interesting and has some sort of emotional hook. The emotional arc drives the rating.

I know that many managers see themselves as data and logic-driven people, not storytellers. But if you want to keep your team performing, you have to get comfortable with telling stories.

––––

Is there a way to get more comfortable with storytelling?

The best advice I can give you to get yourself comfortable with telling stories is to get yourself a journal to record moments that matter. Whenever you have an 'ah-ha' moment associated with the problem you are trying to solve, write it down, then shape it into a short story.

The SBI model is beneficial for simple storytelling:
- Team, I was here (*Situation*);
- I saw x (*Behaviour*);
- and I realised xx; it made me feel like xxx (*Impact*);
- and this is what I want us to now do because of that insight (*Call to action*).

There are some stories I use more than once because of their power. Others I may only use for a conversation with one person.

In the context of keeping the energy up with the team, stop and reflect at the end of that first workshop. What was the vision of the future that got the team excited? Note that down as a memory jogger. Then keep writing down those 'ah-ha' moments to use in one-on-one or team meetings.

- Use stories to celebrate achievements in the actions from the workshop.
- Use stories to share your vulnerability about what is hard along the way, but why you remain excited because of the original vision.
- Use stories to give insights into why the action we have chosen will work.
- Use stories to give insights into why an action will not work and what different action could look like.

Each time you want to get the point across with the team, and keep the energy going, do not just think about data, think about the story behind it. What is the hook that gets people involved?

Be aware that it does not mean that you can tell one story and all of a sudden everyone is optimistic and curious. In a good space, people can remain negative about particular situations. My recommendation is a walk in their shoes. If they are negative, they are in a space where the cortisol is flooding them and whatever is going on is causing them uncertainty, unease, or the sense of a threat. You then need to ask yourself what stories you can tell to trigger oxytocin and make them feel safe. How do you get that connection going through a story? How do you get people being curious through a story?

Never give up on connection and curiosity; they are two critical parts of that mental health pie. And a great story hooks us into them.

————

How do I hold to account the individual team members who are not engaging in problem-solving?

One of the most common frustrations that I have heard from managers is, 'Why do the team not do what they should be doing? Why do they not hold themselves to account?' As senior managers, we would all love it if people had the same level of drive as we did. But they do not. You need to adjust for this reality.

As we have talked about earlier, negativity breeds negativity unless you can break the cycle with curiosity. People cannot shift suddenly from negative to positive, but a shift from negative to *curious* is possible. From there, solving an issue through curiosity can enable a change from curious to positive. It gives them the momentum to get going with the next problem to solve. The critical role that you have as a manager is making sure that you find a way through the first big problem so that the team feel a sense of success. If you let actions slide and expect everyone to hold themselves to account without follow up, you risk breeding cynicism that is harder to repair.

To do this, ask yourself whether every one of these steps are in place:
1. Is everyone crystal clear on the actions that they need to complete? Use SMART (specific, measurable, actionable, realisable, and time-bound) goals to make sure that people are clear on what they need to do and get them to confirm back with you.

2. Are they capable of those actions? Do they have the skill set to follow through on those actions, or do they need some coaching from you to be able to build the skillset? If they are not capable, you cannot expect them to deliver.
3. Are those actions measurable? You need to be able to track progress. In theory from step one, you should have clear actions you can hold them to account on. Grey areas that cannot be measured cause challenges.
4. Are you giving them regular feedback, so they know how they are going and that you are paying attention? When you are busy, it is easy to let things fall off the wagon. They fall off the wagon because if you do not pay attention to it, no one else will see this as a priority focus.
5. Are you acknowledging when they achieve their commitments? Are you discussing next steps when they do not achieve their commitments? If there is not a clear consequence for doing or not doing something, then why would they make it a priority?

You may be feeling that sense of frustration because it is hard work trying to hold everyone to account. If you can keep focusing on those questions above, you will find that you need to do less and less as time goes on. Your teams need guardrails and feedback, to create certainty, and certainty creates a safe environment. As a leader, your role is to provide this environment to enable the brains of your team members to slow down their 'hunt for threats' and be open to solving problems. Create security through certainty and connection, then trigger curiosity— The magical formula that creates a mentally healthy workplace.

———

Key things to remember

- Curiosity is incredibly valuable, both to the individuals and the teams to consistently deliver.
- Get the team curious on what is and is not present that helps build a mentally healthy culture with a brilliant harmonious song.
- Apply a simple process—one problem, three steps, three months and hold the team accountable to these actions then build from there.
- You need to tell captivating stories that keep the team connected to the direction you want them to head in and energised for the journey.

It can be overwhelming at times because of organisational cultural challenges, and you can feel unconvinced that you can make a real change. If you are stuck in the space of negativity, I recommend you go back to Chapter Four and have a look at your mental health pie. What else can you do to get yourself back into the driver's seat? It is only then that you are capable of helping your team get in their driver's seat, which then enables you to create a mentally healthy workplace collectively.

Life does throw us curve balls though. So, in the next chapter, we will explore some of the more common curve balls that can slide a team member closer to red on that continuum. When they are in that space, a team-based methodology will not work. It is time to manage the crisis. Then return to the team-based problem-solving.

CHAPTER EIGHT

CRISIS MANAGEMENT

As a leader, no matter how good you think you are, no matter how well you are working on your mental health to keep yourself mostly in the green, now and again you are going to get hit with a crisis. That is the nature of leading people. You think everything is going smoothly and then one of your team members slides to orange or even to red. You now have an awareness of keeping an eye out for those unexpected changes in people—the subtle changes in mood, mood swings, withdrawal, out of context anger or anxiety that signals something is not quite right. I have seen managers go into a panic, asking, 'What do I do? I am not a psychologist!' You're not expected to be a psychologist, but don't underestimate the power of connection to help the individual as well as the team around them. Your leadership and ability to connect through a crisis will be closely watched and assessed by your team. It is during times of crisis that your team get to see the 'real' you. How you respond in difficult times shows far more about who you are than when times are easy.

Back in Chapter Two, we talked about how important connection is to survival. Remember, Maslow got it wrong? Connection is right up there with food and water as a basic ingredient of our survival.

If someone is seriously struggling, their brain is not coping in the way that your brain would when you are in green, or even in yellow.

The negative classroom inside the head is loud and continually seeing a pattern of threat where a pattern may not exist. The chemicals are out of whack. The person cannot process things in the same way. They can get stuck in a dangerous downward spiral because of it. If they are in the red, they need far more than just connection at work to help bring them back, but not having a connection at work makes it far worse.

Connection in itself cannot prevent the crisis. But it is in these crises that the work that you have done prior on connection makes such a huge difference to recovery.

The strength of the connection that you have with others will be a critical determinant of how you and those around you get through any crisis. Connection makes it easier to manage the situation and dramatically lessens its impact and longevity.

We will start by walking through the practical things you can do to help find signs that might indicate a slide down the continuum.

Then we will explore four common challenges that leaders find themselves faced with:
• performance management issues clouded with mental health issues

- a mental health issue arising within a worker's compensation claim
- realising someone is seriously unwell or potentially suicidal
- recognising when the crisis is you sliding into the orange or red.

You do not need to be a psychologist to connect with someone when they are in orange. From all you have learnt so far, you now have a range of tools in your toolkit to help to build connections with people. If you have put in the work from the previous chapters, then this is where it pays off. You can help a team member get back into yellow and then into green.

If you wait until someone is entirely in crisis to try and connect, it is harder to establish the connection.

If you have not genuinely shown care until someone is in crisis, the most common response of the person in crisis is one of doubt or scepticism.

'You never cared before, why do you suddenly care now? Perhaps it's only because of the impact on your bottom line.' What you need to remember is that when someone is in crisis, there is a high level of cortisol in their body. They are feeling threatened, and any action can be misinterpreted as a further threat. They are not going to see your support in the same way if you have not previously connected. They are likely to be suspicious. Do not lose sight of this. Build a connection *now* before you need it in a crisis.

———

What should I look for to understand whether someone is sliding down the continuum?

Let's think about the SBI feedback model that you learnt to apply in Chapter Six. A period of crisis is when it shows its strengths. I had a team member who was particularly energetic and came into work one day being less enthusiastic than usual. Being able to say, 'I could not help but notice that when you walked in this morning (*Situation*), you were not smiling at everyone and you have been very quietly sitting at your desk. (*Behaviour*). That is not how you normally behave, and that makes me worried (*Impact*). Let's go for a walk (*Call to action*).' This is an excellent way to check-in and work out what is happening.

In that example, I had known that person for long enough to know that their behaviour appeared different. That is the best way to be able to pick up a slide down the continuum—get to know your team members and their typical behaviour. This way, you can pick up any change and talk to them. Remembering it is not the behaviour itself; it is the *change* in behaviour. The loud, funny person who stops contributing to the discussion, the quiet person who suddenly gets angry or the person who refuses to let go of an issue that occurred days or weeks ago. The change is the key, not the actual behaviour.

I encourage you also not just to ask, 'Are you ok?' as it can invite a closed response of 'Yes'. Instead, when you can say, 'I am worried', and you create the time to go for that walk or have a drink together, you invite more. Indeed, silence, after you start the walk or drink, is an excellent way to get them to fill the void.

In the context of a new team member, who you are still getting to know, it is harder. I encourage you to focus on connecting as much as possible to understand how they work. In these early days, you will not know what precisely is 'normal' or 'not normal' for them, but you can still look for responses to issues that seem out of kilter to the event itself. That is either a sense of overthinking a minor issue or brushing off a significant issue. I remember a team member who early on showed a pattern of not keeping a poker face when something was not quite right. When I questioned her without the SBI framework, she would say she was fine, which closed down the conversation. It took feedback with the SBI model a couple of times to start to get her to unlock what was going on with her. It went along the lines of: 'We have just talked about x (*Situation*), I saw your lips tighten, and you looked down at your paper, but when I asked if you were ok you said, 'I'm fine' (*Behaviour*). I am not convinced that you are fine, and that makes me feel concerned that maybe you do not feel like you can be honest with me (*Impact*). So please help me understand what is going on for you right now' (*Call to action*). The SBI model is valuable to use if you do not think the other person is ok. The key, as always, is to call out the impact on *you*—express your concern and how it is affecting you to open up the conversation.

It is as simple as:
- We were talking about this (*Situation*);
- You did/said this (*Behaviour*);
- I am worried about you (*Impact*);
- Let's have a chat. Help me understand what is going on for you. Help me understand how I can help. (*Call to action*).

'Are you okay' is easier to shut down. Using the SBI model above enables the team member to feel like you do see them.

There are times when team members may not want to talk about what is going on for them. You cannot push them into revealing what is happening, but you can keep opening the door to them through this feedback model. Remember, if you want to get the best from people, you need to connect. If you can build a

Building the connection that enables you to spot problems early

My first recommendation is to do a weekly team check-in. This is like the classic safety share; however, it just becomes a well-being share instead. Explain it is important at the beginning of each week to know what is going on for people and how they are feeling. It can be as simple as 'Name the emoji that best represents you today,' to a short description. In my current team, we started this with, 'Choose a word or emoji that best describes you right now'—soon expanding to a short description that the whole team find very useful. There is bonding over late nights, sick babies, life-threatening illnesses, relationship breakdowns, renovations and all sorts of other things. In other words, the team are comfortable to share 'life happens' moments with each other and then say how they feel—calm, in control, energised, tired, overwhelmed, focused, or whatever the description. This technique will enable you to get a read each week on who is in good energy space, who is flagging a bit and who needs help. The more time goes on, the more the team will get comfortable in being vulnerable with each other about how they are feeling. This is not about spending half the meeting on this topic. When the team get into a rhythm, it does not take a long time. But it is powerful information and a great way to focus each week. It only takes one person prepared to be completely vulnerable about how they are feeling and everyone responding positively and with support for people to see the power of admitting when they are struggling.

My second recommendation is getting comfortable with the SBI model. If you keep using it on the small things that build trust, it enables you to then ask about the much bigger things.

Thirdly, watch for change. If someone is already quiet, the fact that they are quiet and withdrawn is not necessarily a problem. Look for those signals that maybe they have slipped a bit further down that continuum. It is the change which is the significant thing—the quiet person suddenly getting angry or upset, the loud and energetic person suddenly becoming withdrawn, the person having an out of context reaction in a meeting. Watch for those changes and then use that SBI model again. This model is essential to build that sense of connection in crisis.

connection and talk about something that is minor or does not seem quite right, you create the trust that enables you to support more effectively if a crisis comes along.

And the more you do it, the more the team will learn to do it with each other as well.

The more team members you have a quality connection with during a crisis, the better off the team will be.

――――――

What if I am performance managing someone and they say they have a mental illness?

I want to talk about performance management and a mental ill-health issue getting 'mixed up' together. It is a common experience that managers come to me for advice. Go back to the first principle—the stronger you build the connection, before any performance issues arise, the greater your ability to avoid problems in the first place.

If you wait until there is a performance management issue to start trying to have an honest conversation, it is a harder road to create that sense of connection given the level of cortisol for that person.

When managers seek advice from me about this type of problem, I can see it is a classic chicken-and-egg issue. What came first, the performance issue or the mental ill-health issue? A common comment is: 'Everything was fine, then all of a sudden they are saying they have got a mental ill-health problem, but it was only after I started to put pressure on them from a performance point of view.' At times, the manager's view underlying this can be either 'I do not believe them' or 'This is frustrating as it gets in the way of the performance management'.

From the team member's perspective, there could be any number of reasons why they have not mentioned mental ill-health to their manager earlier:

1. They have been struggling with their mental health but have not felt connected and safe enough with their manager to open up. Inevitably, untreated issues start to cause performance issues.
2. They know they are not capable of doing the job or feel confused about what is required of them, but have not felt enough connection with their line manager to seek the support they need. This stressful situation then triggers a slide down the continuum, due to lack of clarity or capability in the first place and an inability to connect—worsening performance issues.

3. There is something else going on outside work that is impacting performance at work, but they do not feel safe or connected with their manager to open up. Thereby distracting them and causing performance issues.
4. They did not realise they were not performing until their manager talked to them. They felt fine until they suddenly realised, they were being performance managed. They do not feel a connection with their line manager due to lack of prior feedback, and they slide down the continuum as their brain rightly picks up a 'threat'.

See a pattern here?

It is not the performance itself but the lack of connection that causes the challenge in addressing performance.

Whether the slide down the continuum was already there or the performance review triggered it, what you have is someone with a 'threat' reaction to what is happening. Cortisol is running rife, and they cannot hear you clearly.

If you are not feeling confident about what you are trying to do and you are not getting enough feedback and encouragement, or a sense of confidence, the cortisol gets hold of you. You go into a downward spiral of lack of confidence.

It is essential to understand this pattern as what I often see happening is managers or their HR advisors saying, 'This person has a mental health condition; therefore, we cannot have a conversation with them until they have a medical clearance.' It ends up in this vicious cycle because then the business is waiting until the person is ready to have a conversation about performance. The person knows that is what is going to happen, which makes their mental health worse. They do not want to come back and face the issues. Pulling away and standing in these opposite corners can increase the cortisol for both parties. It certainly causes a deterioration in the relationship, and can cause irreparable damage.

The first step is to get the connection back on track, enabling you to have reasonable conversations about performance. If you just focus on a 'process' and not establish a connection first. The 'process' will not be effective.

I remember one particular case in which I was asked to talk to a senior person in an organisation, who had some serious mental health issues. I experienced some cynicism from those who asked me to talk to her. They were not convinced this person had a mental health problem. They thought that it was 'conveniently' raised.

When I sat down and had a chat with this person, it was apparent to me that she was at least in orange. Just stopping to listen to her, I could see there was a combination of issues. She was particularly focused on what was going on outside of work because she did not want to acknowledge some of the pressures and challenges inside work. From my perspective, they were both causing her to sit in orange—I would say she was in pretty dark orange. My focus with her was to convince her to get professional help as she was too far down the continuum. It took a few follow-ups to convince her to seek help. But eventually, she started seeing a good psychologist with whom she felt a connection. This was the starting point of bringing her back on track.

The response from her manager was to suggest she take time off until she was well enough to face what was happening at work. My suggestion was that she needed to stay connected with work; she needed to feel a sense of self-worth in what she was doing to get back to green. Her confidence had taken a hit, and contribution at work would be a significant contributing factor to her recovery.

I suggested they could still have an honest conversation with her around performance, but in a way where they were able to recognise her strengths and what she could do well. They could explore the reasons that she was not on top of her game at that moment. They could not just say she was no good and performance manage her out of the organisation. She had so much more to give and had demonstrated that previously. She just needed to be in the right setting with the right support. I spent far more time with the manager than I did with her, to help them think about the right conversations. This culminated in both parties agreeing to shift her role on a trial basis and revisit. The new role played to her strengths. Underneath it appeared she was not set up for success with the current role. It took outside help, good connected conversations and her going into another position. The managers could then see how skilled she was and how useful this skillset was. Both the team member and the organisation benefited.

The basic premise is that people do not come to work to do a bad job. Something goes haywire that causes poor performance. It is your role as the leader to build a connection with your team—enabling you to help individual team members explore what may have caused deterioration. This does not mean every situation will end up like the one above. I have had many a conversation where the right decision was the team member leaving and finding an organisation as well as a role that better suited them. The ideal though is that connection helps them be honest and make the call themselves.

———

Should I keep in touch when someone in my team is not well?

One thing that I do find frustrating is managers thinking they cannot contact someone if they are off work with mental illness. This idea has been influenced by the position that sick leave is a right, and when people are sick, they should be left alone to recover. I support that in the context of a serious illness where the person needs to focus on recovery. They need rest. They do not need a call from their manager every second day, asking when they are coming back to work. That kind of pressure is not useful. However, when someone is unwell, it is valuable for them to know that their manager cares about them. It is even more critical if they have slid down the continuum. If they are feeling vulnerable, and they are not getting much contact from people at work, they can misinterpret that silence. They can feel forgotten and neglected. The classroom inside their head becomes increasingly negative. If work factors influenced the slide down the continuum, then maintaining or re-establishing that connection is a vital part of recovery. We all need to know that people at work care for us, that it is a place where we belong.

The key thing is not to assume that what you think is the right connection for you is right for someone else. Work out what works best for each individual, so that they can use connection as part of their recovery.

If someone spirals quickly down into the dark orange or red, it can be tough to build that connection because they are in such a panicked or depressed mode. They may feel at that point that they need to have distance, which may or may not be the right thing for their recovery. In that case, I would recommend reaching out to their emergency contact. They may not know you, but let them know you are reaching out to say, 'We care. Can we talk about how we maintain that connection and how to support?' It means you are keeping that conversation going to help recovery. Even attempts at contact make a difference. The critical principle, however, is to create a connection before performance issues arise.

Just because someone is saying or showing that they have slid down the continuum, it does not mean that you do not face into performance. But you must work out first how to establish a sense of connection between you. Go back to the four perspectives mentioned at the beginning of the chapter to reflect on which situation it might be for this person. A good start is acknowledging things are tough for them right now and that you want to work out what has caused it so you can understand how best to support them.

Sometimes, the person is simply mismatched to the job and sometimes to the organisation. In these cases, it is better for that person's mental health for them to move on. But it may take some time for them to realise. How you treat the person during that process is essential, not just to that person's recovery, but to how everyone else in the team views you as a leader. If you treat them with fairness, respect and a sense of compassion, you will build trust and credibility with your team through that process.

What if there is a worker's compensation claim and someone then slides into orange or red?

What do you think is the most common feeling when someone injures themselves at work? Outside of feeling the pain associated with the direct injury, it is invariably embarrassment. Embarrassment at having to admit they have hurt themselves, that they had to receive treatment in front of others, and the impact their absence will have on others. What do you think is the strongest indicator of whether the person will successfully return to their pre-injury work? It has nothing to do with the severity of the initial injury. It has everything to do with their relationship with their direct manager. Surprise, surprise! Connection rears its head yet again.

I want you to use all that you have learned thus far in this book to think about what it might be like for someone injured at work. To help you, I want you to think about you rolling your ankle badly when exercising. After the initial pain of the first 24 hours settles down, you are left with a list of things you cannot do—you are advised you have to be on crutches for a couple of weeks. You cannot drive; support your team through to finals; go on that motorbike ride you had planned. The family wedding in the gardens you are attending becomes a challenge because there are no chairs. The list goes on. You cannot afford to catch cabs to work. So, you are missing out on what is happening. There is a team building day at work, and you cannot participate—and no one calls. The classroom inside your head kicks in. There is the frustration of not being able to do things that is coupled with the feeling of isolation—then hurt, when no one contacts you to keep you in the loop.

Elizabeth Kubler-Ross is a world-renowned psychiatrist who developed the five stages of grief model. From denial to anger, bargaining, depression, and finally, acceptance. While this model was designed in the context of understanding how humans process the death of a loved one, it is just as applicable to any loss. The depth and duration of each phase may vary, and people may move back and forth between these phases depending on circumstances. Still, the model is a helpful one to understand what happens when someone processes grief. When you are injured, you have lost some part of you. If you are injured *outside* work through your chosen activities, your anger and frustration is more likely to be directed at yourself. When someone is injured at work, this anger and frustration can be directed towards the workplace or even particular people.

It is natural with all this going on, that people will not be sitting in the green after they are injured at work.

The classroom inside that person's head could include some of the following questions or thoughts:
- I cannot believe I am missing out on 'xx'. It's not fair.
- I cannot concentrate on anything. I hate this pain.
- Why can't it be better now?
- I do not know how I could do my work.
- My manager only seems to care about when I can return to work. They have no idea how this has affected me.
- I thought I had friends at work, but everyone seems too busy to care about me.

As the classroom inside their head becomes more negative, they are automatically in the yellow. Remember we are pattern-seeking creatures. If we feel like we are not supported or cared for, then everything we see people do will be interpreted with this belief in mind. Our brain is processing it as a threat. In comes the cortisol.

I have seen this time and time again working in the workers' compensation arena. Once someone is injured at work, they can feel worried about coming back to work. They can feel stressed about what their team thinks of them—Whether they are going to be accepted or whether they are going to be able to do their job because of the injury. Cortisol runs rife. It has little to do with the severity of the injury and everything to do with how they feel about work and their relationships with work. In particular, their relationship with you as their line manager. What I see then is managers making it worse through a lack of attempts at connection, while only following a 'process'. They are focused on their frustrations and managing tasks at work and the impact to them, *not* the injured person.

You need to do what you can to stop them from sliding into the orange or red. A slide into the orange or red is a high price to pay at an individual and organisational level. When a team member is injured, that classroom can be so loud, that they are unable to bring themselves back without help. As the line manager, you play the most critical role in helping the person through the injury and recovery as fast as possible. How? You guessed it, through connection.

I do not expect any manager to be an expert in workers compensation; that is for your insurer and return to work expert. However, you do need to become an expert at connecting with people. The sense of connection that the individual feels towards you as their manager is the single best predictor of a successful outcome. If the person is feeling connected to you as a manager, they are going to want to get back to work as quickly as possible. If they feel they are part of a connected team, they will want to get back into that team as soon as possible. The pull of connection is what gets a much better outcome.

If you find yourself tomorrow with an injured team member, before you have had a chance to build connection, then my recommendation is to start with vulnerability. Be able to say:

'I have reflected on what I have failed to do, which is to make sure I have connected with you to make sure you are part of the team. I am sorry that it is you being injured that has made me realise my failure. I want to make it up to you now by doing what I can to help you feel supported and part of the team while you recover. Let's talk about how I do this on a practical basis...'

This is even more critical when it is a psychological claim. The person can be feeling so overwhelmed with cortisol that they believe not talking to people at work is the best option. Yet it is connection not detachment that helps recovery. Even if that connection, to begin with, is tenuous. You need to find whatever way possible to re-establish the connection. This is what is critical to the business and the recovery of the person off work. Start with trying to do it yourself directly. If this fails, it might work through a work colleague they trust. It may be through an independent professional. The key point—never give up on building the connection.

The less time we spend on connection up front, the more energy and time we end up spending on following a 'process'. People get so focused on both sides on liability decisions, or rights, or the next step in the process. That is missing the point. A connection is what gets both parties to a better outcome—not a process. The process can increase cortisol levels, while connection decreases cortisol.

———

What if I believe someone is really in the dark red zone?

If someone is rapidly deteriorating from orange to red, this is one of the scariest things to see as a line manager. It is your strength of connection with that person that can assist them in getting help as quickly as they can. This is not a guaranteed recipe for success, but it is your best chance to assist.

You need to remember that if someone is spiralling into red, their ability to speak rationally about their situation is often curtailed. They might think that they are rational, due to not seeing a different perspective at that point, but they are not thinking in the same way as you are. I have heard people describe feeling suicidal as most of the brain shutting down and seeing life through a pinhole. They cannot see much light at all, and they cannot see beyond current challenges. The 'person' which, to me, is the presence behind the thoughts and feelings, is trapped by a brain's negative thought processes and emotions. Just like diseased cells can multiply and take over the physical body, so too do the automatic negative thoughts and cortisol take over the brain.

If they are in red, you, as the line manager, will not be able to pull them back on your own. No one can. They need serious medical help to return from that. The best you can do is get them the help that they need. How? Through your connection. You can keep them talking to you, so you can then 'lead' them to the people and supports that can help.

What if someone tells me they are thinking of taking their life?

If you are in a conversation with someone who expresses that life is not worth living or they think they might kill themselves, do not ignore or brush over this. You need to step into the conversation with direct questions to keep them talking so you can work out how quickly help is required. You can start the conversation with a version of the SBI. Skip the situation component as it is in the here and now. You can jump to:

'Can I pause for a moment. You have just said xxx, and that makes me feel worried about you.' Then you can go into further questions.

'Tell me about it, have you thought about the method by which you are going to kill yourself?' Although this sounds very confrontational, it can help you ascertain if they are in imminent danger.

If they say they haven't thought about a method, it can indicate a call for help rather than imminent danger. At this point you say something like:

'While we sit here, let's get someone on the phone who can help you. Tell me about a close family member or friend I can call'. If they don't believe they have anyone, then help them get professional help through either your own company Employee Assistance Program (EAP) or through an external agency set up to support people in crisis.[*]

If you are face to face with a team member who has expressed these thoughts, it is easier to keep them safe with you while you call for help. If you are on the phone to them, and they have indicated they have a thought about a method, you can keep them talking through asking further questions, such as:

'Have you got the equipment to do that?'

'When are you planning to do that?'

The person who can answer these questions is at risk right now. So, you want to get them both professional help and social support as soon as possible.

At this point, while keeping contact with them, ring emergency services to get them into medical care before they harm themselves. Also communicate with their emergency contact to get them social support.

Is it normal to feel scared?

Yes, is the answer to that question.

It is common for managers to think:
- 'I am not a psychologist. I do not think I can do this.'
- 'What if I say the wrong thing?'

---

[*] In Australia call Lifeline on 13 11 14 or help this person to a local medical clinic.

Many organisations are investing in mental health first aid training as a way of getting people prepared to respond to these situations—this is valuable training for any manager. Beyond Blue also has excellent resources, providing you with further information in this area.*

Remember that the underlying principle is connection. You may not use the exact words I have, but the underlying principle behind them is establishing if this person is at risk right now. The greater risk is saying nothing. It is far better to come in with some questions, even if it is a bit clunky than to stay silent and ignore the warning signs.

Using this process does not guarantee that person will not attempt to end their life. Not all suicides are preventable. For some people sadly, the illness has taken over to the point there is nothing you could have done. This, in itself, can slide you into orange. Hence the importance of you always having a strong mental health pie and seeking your own professional support if needed. But do not underestimate the power of being able to ask these questions.

When I have rolled out mental health first aid training, I have received consistent positive feedback on the confidence this gave managers to step into this situation and help get people the support they need. They feel like very direct questions to ask, but this is a human to human response and the training can increase people's confidence. This training is not the answer to mental health in the workplace, but it can be a valuable component. If someone is in trouble, connection is what helps to get them the support they need. Get familiar with the questions. If you are feeling a bit worried, take those questions, put them on a laminated card and stick them in your back pocket or your wallet, so it is handy. Just get famil-

---

* https://www.beyondblue.org.au/the-facts/suicide-prevention/worried-about-some-one-suicidal/having-a-conversation-with-someone-you're-worried-about

iar with those questions and know that they are ready to use if you need them.

———

How can I stop the crisis from being me?

I have seen too many managers who have fallen apart and have ended up taking extended time off and career breaks because they took too long to recognise the signs. They were ignoring what their bodies were telling them. Remember what I said in Chapter Two. You think you are in control, but you are not when you have gone down the continuum. Your brain is pretty smart, and your body is trying to signal to you that things are not great.

Be mindful of any changes in your pattern of behaviour. If you can see you are not sleeping as well, you are not eating well, you are starting to drink excessively, you are not doing the exercise that you should be doing, and your emotions are all over the place, stop and reflect. What does this say about where you are on the continuum? What needs strengthening in your pie?

If you feel like you have slipped down the continuum, and your pie is not working to bring you back, then seek help through your connections. Is it from family, friends, a professional, or all three? The critical thing is to identify you are slipping down the continuum, recognise this, use the levers within the pie, and if at this point it is not enough, seek professional help. We are all human and just like with physical health, we can become susceptible to certain illnesses where professional help is the best outcome. If you are concerned that you have experienced suicidal thoughts, feelings or distress and are worried they may come back, I recommend an app called *Beyond Now* from Beyond

Blue. This app enables you to create a plan with a health professional, or someone in your support network, to help if suicidal thoughts enter your head.

————

Key things to remember

- As a manager, you will get hit with a variety of different crises, and the strength of connection you have with others will be the crucial determinant of how you get through it.
- Your work on connection enables you to detect problems earlier on and address them before they escalate.
- It is usual for people to feel anxious and 'fall apart' when initially facing performance management or they are injured or ill. Your role is to understand what is contributing to the slide down the continuum and where you can help versus where they need to own it.
- If someone says they do not think life is worth living, do not brush it aside. Ask more questions to understand whether this is an immediate risk or not, and help them get support. They are stuck in red at that point.
- You are vulnerable too, so you need to keep watching yourself and asking for help where needed.

Connection is what we are trying to achieve, and it is hard. It does not happen automatically. Yet, it unlocks so much of the individual's health, and the team and company's performance.

If you are always looking for the 'strongest' and 'toughest' people to do things, you are missing out on some of the best skills to get you the results that you want.

The ones who are 'strong', ironically, often struggle with connection to others, because they have put up such a mask that they are not able to connect effectively. This lack of connection to self will not assist them to thrive in the complex world ahead, nor get the best from their teams. Keep persevering with connection, it is worth it and will help you through any crisis.

This is almost the end of the book. In our next chapter, we are going to look at how we tie it all together and make it click so it can be life-changing for you and the way that you lead your team.

CHAPTER NINE

IS IT STICKY ENOUGH?

In this last chapter, I want to focus on the tools that help you make it stick. That makes the mental health pie part of your team habit with you as the expert musical director of the song of culture sustaining a mentally healthy workplace. That is the sweet spot—everything is built into a habit—It is sticky. When it is sticky, you do not need as much energy to keep it going. If you do not keep connecting with the team and with yourself, and contributing and staying curious, you will not maximise your mental health and performance for the organisation.

There are four techniques that I want to focus on to help build the habits. One from each component of the pie which help make it sticky.

First, I want to talk about journaling, which is all about connecting with yourself. Then we will talk about key connections with

How much pie do I need today?

others who keep you on track. Next, we will talk about the habit of processing failure, which is about curiosity. Then we will finish with giving back—your contribution.

———

Why should I buy a journal?

Journaling is a circuit breaker for our brain. I have talked about how it is hard to think logically when the cortisol is running through your brain. Journaling is giving the brain an activity to distract it. Getting those thoughts out on paper helps you in the moment as a form of distraction and enables you to process what the classroom inside your head is trying to tell you.

I started journaling when I was at school. Back then, as the typical anguished teenager, I found getting my thoughts down on paper a good way to distance myself from intense emotions. I continued through the university years of 'finding myself' and into my management roles. Still, it was not until I hit challenging times as a manager that I started to appreciate the value of a journal. It enabled me to release emotions and to get perspective. I could look back on older journals and realise the perspective I had gained over time. It also helped me capture the amazing highs, reflect on what I was grateful for, and capture inspiring quotes to keep me going. These entries I can still read back on and smile.

I did wonder whether it was just me who valued a journal. I googled, 'Why is writing a journal good for you?' and was fascinated by how many articles with research supporting the importance of journaling came up. Articles I found included 'The 83 Benefits of Journaling for Depression, Anxiety, and Stress 'from *Positive Psychology*, 'Journaling for Mental Health' from the Rochester University and '10 Surprising Benefits You'll Get From Keeping a Journal' from the *Huffington Post*. Consistently, both university-based research and organisations associated with wellbeing support the value of journaling for our mental health.

Journaling is not necessarily an everyday task, although some people like the regularity of doing so. I would encourage using a journal at least monthly, if not weekly. It is a way of strengthening the connection to self in your mental health pie.

I am sure you have all heard of the recommendation that if you are angry about an email you have received, write a response email but do not send it. Then go back the next day and read it and remember why it is valuable not to send that email. A journal is just like those draft emails. You just keep them for future reflection to continue to learn and strengthen your pie.

What if I am no good at writing?

If you are thinking you are no good at writing things down or do not know where to start, a key thing to remember is that no one else is reading it. There is no judgement from anyone other than yourself. It does not matter whether you think it is sub-standard to begin with or not, just focus on writing in a way that helps you— not on what is insightful or useful to someone else.

The other key thing is to do it your way. Just start. It could be dot points, it could be a mind map, or it could be just random thoughts. It could be random words about how you are feeling about something. If you like drawing, it might be a drawing. It can be anything. It is simply a way for you to get what is going on in your head down on paper. What you are trying to do is calm that classroom inside your head.

If you find you forget to do it, find a way to work it into your routine. To begin with, set aside some time in your schedule. It could be daily, weekly or monthly. Maybe leave your journal and pen next to your bed to prompt reflection at the end of the day. Leaving the journal where you keep seeing it is a good reminder.

Once you start feeling the benefit of regular journaling, you will find it becomes easier to do. Remember, if you are motivated to do something, you naturally find time to do it. If it is a habit, you will not even think about it. You will just do it.

While journaling is an excellent tool, if you are feeling that you are slipping into the orange or beyond on the continuum, then

Getting over writer's block with a journal

Buy a good quality journal. You want to enjoy even opening it up. (or maybe that is just me). Outside of mind maps and dot points, here are some questions/prompts that might help you when you do not know where to start. Just choose one to write about each time you pick up your journal.

Connecting to self

- Where am I on the continuum today?
- Where am I on the energy scale today?
- This month, my mental health pie looks like…
- This is what went well today…
- How have I looked after myself today?

Connecting to others

- Who have I connected with today? How did that make me feel?
- My reflection on an SBI feedback I gave is… [what I think worked well or did not]

Contribution

- Who have I helped today? How?
- Who have I made sure felt valued today? How?

Curiosity

- What have I learnt today?
- What conversation loops are stuck in the classroom inside my head today?
- What emotion seems to keep bubbling up to the surface for me today?

These are all ways of bringing what you have been doing within your mental health pie to your conscious mind. You will see that they connect back to the exercises in Chapter Five. You may want to go back to those exercises and complete one or more of them in your journal each month.

please seek external help. Journaling will be a useful ongoing tool, but not on its own in an immediate crisis.

———

Who is on your Board?

Regardless of your role in the company, you are the CEO of your own life. Any good CEO has a good Board around them. Think about it in the context of the work environment. In a well-rounded company Board, you have different 'voices' or expertise from areas such as marketing, risk management, finance, legal, strategy, and people. It is the diversity of experience and perspectives that a company Board has that helps to unlock performance.

So too does the diversity of thought around you enable you to be your best self. It maximises your mental health. I am not suggesting you have a group of people who meet regularly to discuss your mental health and career. But you do need to know who you can turn to for a range of different perspectives to help you move forward.

The concept of having your personal 'Board' is one I wished was introduced far earlier in my career. It is also a concept I introduce to anyone I mentor. I have seen time and again how this Board has helped people get through the tough times and improve.

I am going to take you through the six people or voices you need, outside your head, helping you. Grab that journal and write down your thoughts on who in your life plays these roles as I go through them. As you make those notes remember the diversity of thought and experience is vital. You need different perspectives sitting at your 'table'. No one person can play every role.

1. The Spark

The 'Spark' is the person you go to when you need inspiration and energy about what to do next. They can paint a picture of the future that looks appealing to you when you cannot see the future clearly. They open your eyes to the landscape, to where the opportunities are. They help you generate ideas which give you a path forward. They give you the energy of dopamine.

2. The Strength

This is the person that you go to when you have fallen off your bike. Life has got a little bit tough. You need someone to remind you of what your strengths are, to help get your confidence back. Remember that saying I have repeated again and again, 'I have been seen, I have been heard and I matter'? This is the person who reminds you that you are enough. That regardless of what is currently happening, you are valued and have a valuable contribution to make. They help you back to the green end of the continuum. They give you that warm oxytocin feeling.

3. The Serious

The 'Serious' is the person who cares for you as much as the 'Strength' does, but their part is different. They are the person you want when you are on cloud nine, when you are full of all the best ideas and about to leap off the cliff. They bring you down a peg or two. They are the one who will point out the holes in the road before you fall into them. They do this because they do not want to see you hurt. They are the voice of reason that you do not want to hear when you are on cloud nine but think of them as bringing you back from an extreme green to a balanced green—a healthier balanced perspective. Where you can see the risks and put a plan in place to manage them. They can be frustrating but do play an important role. They will trigger mild cortisol to keep you alert to pitfalls.

4. The Stair Master

As the name suggests, this person is one that keeps you climbing those stairs. You have set yourself a goal, and they are the one who asks, 'How are you going with that?' They are the person who rings you up once a week to find out how the new exercise routine, diet, meditation, hobby, or critical project is going. They keep you accountable to the things that you need to build into a habit. Think of them as your personal trainer. They help you build your pie. They help you stay in green. They help you get the dopamine hit of achievement because they help you stick to your plan and achieve your goals.

5. The Seer

This is your classic mentor and the person that you turn to for sage advice. The person who has been there and done that. You can ask them, 'How did you deal with this stuff? Where do I start? What do I do? Who do I talk to?' You feel valued when someone experienced is willing to spend time with you, which triggers your serotonin.

6. The Silly

This is the voice of laughter that I talked about in Chapter Five. When all else fails, there is extraordinary value in being able to find someone to have an enormous belly laugh with, which triggers your oxytocin.

Remember that you are like anyone else. Regardless of your role, you need connection. We all need connection. As CEO of your own life, you need to get into the driver's seat of creating the connection you need. If you find the right people to have around you, people who truly see you for who you are and what you bring to the table, you have got the best chance of looking after your mental health, having a great career and being able to pay it forward in helping others as well. Your Board helps you make sure your habits stick, because they want to see you succeed, and keep growing.

One of my favourite Sparks is the author Simon Sinek. I love this quote from him: 'Courage comes from the level of support we feel around us.' In the second half of the chessboard that we face, we need courage as leaders to make a difference. But we cannot do that unless we have that great support around us.

Just as the CEO would not look to the marketing person for technical accounting advice, you too need to decide when you are looking for advice, which voice will help you the most in any given situation. Journaling can help you reflect and identify when you need that spark of energy, a reminder of your strengths, the steadying of your energy, focus, wise words or laughter. Seek out the voice that will help you, not the voice that is the easiest to access. This is the way to get the most from your Board.

What to do when you do not have a complete Board

While I have been describing those different roles, hopefully, you have been identifying certain people in your life who fit them, which is excellent. If, however, you are finding that you have got a couple of blank spots, let me get you to think about a few ways of filling in the blanks.

Start with finding your Strength, Serious and Silly outside of the work environment. They are the three that have the greatest sense of connection to who you are. It is crucial for your mental health to ensure you have those voices as a start. Over time you can then build them inside work.

In thinking about who could play the Stair Master, think about one particular part of the pie that you are working on and just focus on a Stair Master for that area. For example, if you want to increase your physical fitness, it could be a personal trainer. If it is diet, it could be a dietician. If it is leadership style, it could be an executive coach.

For the Spark, if you have not got a natural person that you would go to who gives you that energy of inspirational ideas, you might want to start with writers that you feel speak to you. For me, Brené Brown and Simon Sinek are two people that I find give me great energy.

For the Seer, if you do not have a natural mentor, look at what you really want to learn. Do not think about anything and everything, but narrow it down by asking, 'What are the things I want to focus on at the moment?' Instead of looking up, look to your peers inside or outside the organisation. Who are the colleagues who might be able to help you with something that you want to learn right now?

Ultimately, your Board will keep changing as you grow, and as challenges come up. It is essential to regularly check in on whether you need to change the person playing each role on your Board.

What do I do when I fall over?

I want to talk about failure as an opportunity to learn. There are going to be times when you have not looked after yourself—when you have not been able to connect. You will not be happy with your half-baked pie. You may have a crisis that throws the pie out the window. We would all prefer it not to happen, yet it is through our stumbles that we can learn and become stronger for it. At the heart of becoming better as a leader is to stay curious through 'failure'. To be okay with being uncomfortable for a while because you know this is a growing pain.

Keeping curiosity at the forefront of your mind helps to calm the cortisol down when things do not go to plan. It moves the brain from thinking there is a threat to being open to learning. And each little goal you achieve or answer you find along the way gives your brain a kick of dopamine. I love this quote from Brené Brown's book, *Dare to Lead*[*], where she quotes Joseph Campbell saying, "The cave you fear to enter holds the treasure you seek." A good reminder that if you are in the middle of something unpleasant, you can recognise that there is an opportunity to learn.

You cannot stop uncomfortable things from happening, but if you flip your perspective, you will be able to get into the driver's

---

[*] Brown, Brené (2018) Dare to Lead. Vermillion, Penguin Random House, London. UK.

seat and see the opportunity. Always trying to avoid things will create more cortisol for you. It is not a healthy thing to do. It is important to be able to breathe your way through it.

In Chapter Five I talked about having such a difficult time in a workplace that I came close to breaking. It was curiosity that got me through it—I kept coming back to curiosity—challenging myself on what I could learn from an ordinary situation. I used journaling as part of it and kept reminding myself; 'There is something in here that I can learn from and benefit from, what is it?' A key thing I learnt was how critical my mental health pie is to recovery and sustainable health. It was uncomfortable. Some days were tougher than others, and I did not like it. But, I grew as a leader because of it. I am much stronger now because of it. I will continue to fail in the future. But I am better at recognising the growth opportunity and working out how to breathe through it. You will fail too. But if you can learn from those events, you will become much stronger mentally for it. Or as Tony Robbins says, "there is no such thing as failure, only results"[*]. Sure, those results may not have been what you hoped. But they are a great learning opportunity. So, stay curious.

When times are challenging, use your journal and your Board to help process what is happening. Sometimes just writing things down will help you get perspective, other times, you might need help from those different Board members to work out what you can learn from the situation.

If my team members are in the middle of something difficult, one of the actions I ask them to do is to grab a sticky note and write 'Learning happens outside your comfort zone' and stick it on their computer screen. Then I ask them to reflect on which voice they need to hear right now. I recommend you do this too.

---

[*] Robbins, Anthony (1986). Unlimited Power: The New Science of Personal Achievement. Simon and Schuster Ltd. London, UK.

The reflection and the Board are critical, but this small reminder every time you look at the computer can also help you breathe through the situation.

———

How does contributing everyday help stickiness?

The final thing is thinking about how we help people every day. Back when we talked about the mental health pie, one of those components was contribution. Contribution does not necessarily mean helping out at a charity regularly or donating money, albeit they are excellent things to do. Rather it is helping someone each day in some small way. It could be giving recognition for a job well done. It could be a great piece of coaching. It could be showing care by stopping to ask a few questions when you know someone has a personal struggle. Making someone else feel better each day helps your mental health as well as theirs. They feel connected and cared for, eliciting oxytocin for them. You can get a dopamine hit from achieving a small goal you set, and another serotonin hit when you get a positive response from the other person on how much they valued your feedback or assistance. Some of that effect can last for a long time.

Think about how it feels when someone gives you some small piece of positive feedback. At senior levels, we do not get that often. But when we do, how awesome is it to feel that way? Do not underestimate the impact this has on others. When I started a new job, I had to present for half an hour in front of about 400 people. It was my first opportunity to build my profile as a General Manager. My manager was not present, but he came to see me about two hours later and asked, 'How did you think it went?' I responded, 'I think it went okay'. He replied; 'I heard you hit it out of the ballpark. Well done!' With a big grin on his face. It was such a small piece of feedback, and I am sure by now he has probably forgotten that he ever said that, but I will always remember how much I felt my confidence build. He had received feedback from a few people and came to give me that boost soon after I presented, and I could see the impact it had on him. That one piece of feedback spurred me on with our major agenda on safety leadership.

I suggest putting a reminder time slot (not just task) in your diary. 'Who have I helped today?' It is a daily reminder to think about how you are connecting with not just your team but the broader organisation.

Here are some questions that can help prompt you on how you can contribute:

- Who is currently going through a challenging personal time? Can I message, call or talk to them about how they are going?
- Is it someone's birthday I can call?
- Who has exceeded performance targets this week/month that I can recognise using SBI feedback?
- Who has handled a challenging situation well that I can recognise using SBI feedback?
- Who is not performing who I could spend time coaching?
- Who could I spend one-to-one coaching time with on their career?
- What funny story could I share to get someone to laugh?
- What can I do to make sure someone knows how much I appreciate them?

These questions are just prompts to get that brain thinking.

Do not forget that you can, and should, think about contribution outside the workplace as much as you think about it inside the workplace. How can you show a family member or friend how much you appreciate them? How can you offer support to someone close who is struggling?

An outstanding manager of mine introduced me to an exercise that I have used in a number of my team meetings to build up the contribution muscle of mental health. It also builds the energy in a room when you need a focused meeting. I ask the team to line up in two rows facing each other. Then explain, 'You have two minutes to thank each other for something the other person has recently done that has helped you or the team'. It is a form of speed dating. You have the two minutes then you move down the line to give feedback to more people. We just do not stop enough to say thank you. It is simple, powerful and excellent for our mental health.

The level of energy and connection you feel in doing that is amazing. We often think contribution is such a big thing, but it is not. It can be small. But connecting with someone and thanking them comes back to us tenfold. If you want a healthy, happy life, then contributing to others is a crucial part of the pie. Once you start doing it regularly, you will appreciate the chemicals that kick in so much that you will not want to stop. It is addictive and builds your mental health pie—It is worth it.

Conclusion

Imagine a world where, in the war for talent, you win every time.
You win because of how present you are with your mental health.
You win because of how you lead others to look after theirs.

You win because you know how to design the work and workplace to create both challenge and support to get the best results.

Word spreads. You are the leader people want to work with. The depth of connection that comes from authentic, honest, vulnerable conversations, builds a team performance that will outstrip the performance of any competitor. Does it mean no problems? Of course not, that is unrealistic. It is not problem-free, but you have dedicated problem solvers because people who learn and implement the disciplines of the mental health pie, are primed for effective problem-solving. Remember, it is only through true connection that we can unlock our potential as individuals, as teams, as organisations, as the human race.

You need to build a framework of support to make these sticky habits that you want to have in your mental health pie. As Brené Brown said in *Dare to Lead*, 'If you are going to dare greatly, you are gonna get your ass kicked at some point.' And being a leader is all about daring greatly.

So, in preparation for this, you need your mental health pie to be strong:
- Buy that journal and get reflective on your journey so you can stay connected to yourself and what is happening for you physically and mentally.
- Build that brilliant Board and stay connected with them, to help shine the light where you cannot see.
- Expect failure and stay curious to the curveballs so you can keep learning.
- Contribute to others every day in some small way.

As a *Game of Thrones* fan, I am tempted to end with 'Winter is coming', but this is too bleak a perspective. Rather, ongoing change is inevitable. It is through connection that we can bring our best selves to the table to solve the challenges and maximise

the opportunities of the second half of the chessboard.
    You need to look after yourself.
    Then look after the team.
    Then guide the organisation.
    So, let's go make pies.

EPILOGUE

It has taken me some time to realise I have lived most of my adult life with a low level of underlying anxiety. This anxiety has been incredibly helpful in driving me to achieve all the things I have achieved. It has always made me curious to learn more about how this world of ours works and why humans are so complex, yet so simple in their responses to the issues they face. But it has also left me with exhaustion at times, with too much cortisol in my body. It has taken a few serious dips in my overall well-being over my career for me to challenge myself about what routines best serve me for the long run. What I have realised in more recent years, in exploring challenges with a range of senior managers, is that low-level anxiety exists for so many leaders. It helped push us to where we are. But we need to do more to look after this one body and brain of ours as we face the upheaval that a global pandemic and the changes the fourth industrial revolution brings.

When I first wrote this epilogue, it was well before the COVID-19 pandemic, and I included here one of my favourite quotes from the Lord of the Rings. It is no surprise that it has appeared as a rallying cry during the pandemic.

"'I wish it need not have happened in my time' said Frodo. 'So do I' said Gandalf, 'and so do all who live to see such times. But that is not for them to decide. All we have to decide is what to do with the time that is given us.'"[*]

Everyone has been challenged in different ways by the pandemic. But one thing to me is clear. People across the globe have accepted their vulnerability, and are working hard to manage heightened anxiety. I believe that we as leaders play such a vital role in reversing the trend of mental illness and getting our organisations to thrive despite the complexity and lack of certainty in this world. It starts with your internal reflections, builds to helping others in your teams to take that self-responsibility, then turns to learning about the shadow that you cast. Then you can examine how you design the workplace of the future and how you connect in your conversations and through your challenges to get the best sustainable results.

Success in property is all about location, location, location. Sustainable high performing teams are all about connection, connection, connection.

Become part of the worldwide movement of leaders who are taking control of their mental health and guiding their teams to do the same. Become part of my connected community and let us start a conversation on shaping the organisations of the future for the better.

---

[*] Tolkien, J.R.R. (1954) The Fellowship of the Ring – The first part of The Lord of the Rings. George Allen and Unwin. London, UK.

In all of this, we need to put our oxygen masks on first.

From a personal perspective, I share with you with my mental health mantra, which keeps me going:

- Love sleep like I love chocolate.
- Remember to breathe deeply because this moment too shall pass.
- Get moving; it is the best antidepressant.
- Appreciate food, health, family, friends, the sunshine and the rain every day.
- Connect, care, contribute and be curious every day.
- Make a difference in someone else's life every day by helping in some small way to make them feel like they have been seen, they have been heard, and that they matter.
- When all else fails, find laughter with others.

As leaders, we have such a responsibility for how we shape our future world. And so, I leave you with a wonderful saying from Gandhi:

'Be the change you want to see in the world.'

YOUR READY RECKONER

If you are like me, then in reading through this book you may well have already underlined key points and put a few sticky notes in places to remind yourself of things to go back to. To make this a bit easier for you when you want to start doing these exercises with your teams, here is a 'contents' page for those key exercises. When you need a refresher, I would also recommend doing a quick read through 'Key things to remember' at the end of each chapter.

QUICK REFLECTION: Where are you right now? 19

QUICK QUESTIONS: How well do you know your team? 20

FIGURE TWO: The physical health continuum 25

FIGURE THREE: The psychological health continuum 27

PRACTICAL STEPS: Your position on the continuum 29

PRACTICAL STEPS: The impact of your brain's chemicals on you   38

PRACTICAL STEPS: Your day, your week, your month   50

PRACTICAL STEPS: Minimising your negative shadow   68

PRACTICAL STEPS: Quick assessment of culture   82

PRACTICAL STEPS: Is your workplace mentally healthy?   87

PRACTICAL STEPS: Assessing your energy   98

PRACTICAL STEPS: Assessing your mental health pie   102

REMINDER: The SBI feedback model   134

REMINDER: Deciding if your team is ready for team based mental health   158

REMINDER: The team based mental health model   160

PRACTICAL STEPS: Are we a mentally healthy team?   163

REMINDER: Creating accountability   169

PRACTICAL STEPS: Building connection to spot problems   177

REMINDER: The reasons why someone might bring up mental ill health during performance discussions   179

REMINDER: Responding to someone who appears suicidal   189

PRACTICAL STEPS: Getting better at journaling   199

PRACTICAL STEPS: Building your Board   204

ACKNOWLEDGEMENTS

I was lucky enough to be selected in 2017 to participate in the inaugural McKinsey & Company Australian and New Zealand Executive Leadership Program. I can still clearly picture speaking to my mentor Diane Smith-Gander where she challenged me with a great question. 'What will you do to make this opportunity count?' For several years, I had been considering writing a book on how to get people to connect more effectively in order to solve problems. Whether at team, organization, or broader level. My time over the three years of this program, with valuable conversations along the way with incredible leaders across the globe, have kept me determined to have an impact in an area that I am incredibly passionate about: Sustainable performance through connection. For all of what we want to achieve individually, it is the power of the truly connected effort that will enable us to bring our best selves to the table and solve the complex problems the world faces.

So, in the spirit of connection I want to thank some key people who have been influential in getting me started, keeping me going and providing me with the opportunities to experiment with different ways of getting teams to work more effectively together. It is through these opportunities that I have been able to talk about the elephant in the room, our own and each other's mental health.

I am forever grateful to Caroline Cameron who challenged and supported me to find my sense of purpose when I was struggling with burn out many year ago. It was then Terry Bowen, Colin Pavlovich and Andy Coleman whose belief in me enabled me to take all of the struggles of prior roles into significant growth as a leader. Mike Vierow, thank you for having the vision of enabling the future leaders of Australia to truly lead in a complex world that then became the catalyst for finally putting pen to paper. To that end I thank not only Mike, but Leah Weckert who believed in me enough to nominate me for this program and Diane Smith-Gander for not only challenging me to do something with the opportunity but for always believing in me and pushing me to do more. There were so many inspirational leaders I met during the program but I do want to call out Tom Harkin, Claire Goodson and Alis Anagnostakis for always providing different thought-provoking perspectives on how this world operates. To the beautiful Georgie Harman, thank you for encouraging me to keep going in challenging times. I am also indebted to Jennifer Westacott who reminded me more than once to do what I love rather than chase a position. Doing what I love includes much reading in the arena of leadership and mental health. It is only through 'standing on the shoulders of giants' that this book has come about so thank you to those giants. I hope that I have reflected on your work accurately to build insights.

To the many leadership teams and leaders I have worked with over the years, thank you for putting up with my experimentation, curiosity and forever challenging 'the way we do things', with a particular call-out to my Coles #dreamteam in safety and wellbeing who were with me all the way when I launched the mental health program at Coles well before its time. And to Emma Bridges who was truly that first follower. I am so lucky to have worked with you. To Kath Walters and her 90-day book coaching program, without which this book never would have been written, thank you for emulating challenging AND supportive feedback. To Lu Sexton, thank you for the initial editing that convinced me to keep going. I am also appreciative of those that read my book in this early format and gave me the encouragement to keep going and with great challenges. I particularly want to call out Chris Tabois, David Venour, Leonie Green and Georgie Harman. Without your words of wisdom and encouragement I may not have got to the finish line and certainly would not have got there in the time I had originally planned to! And to the amazing team at ckaos who were so patient, focused, warm and encouraging which enabled the book to be ready for publishing. I could not have done this without you.

On a personal level, a huge thank you to Steve, Natasha and Lawrence, my beautiful family who put up with me using any spare minute on a weekend in front of the laptop writing rather than spending time with them and debating those final decisions with me on the book design. Without your laughter, support, tolerance and energy, this book would not have been possible. A call out also to my MOMs group (aka Meeting of the Minds). I am aware of how lucky I am to be one of nine children. But even luckier to have the connection I have with my older brother Andrew and my younger sister Leonie who know me so well. You challenge me to stay real. You always give direct, honest brilliant SBI feedback. You pick me up when I am wobbly and help me dust myself off. You never fail to make me laugh, feel joy and appreciate life. And lastly to my incredible 87-year-old mum who I swear gets younger every day. She is the living proof of what great connection can do to enable you to lead a fulfilling, happy life. Many years ago, mum told us her philosophy on life. Never stop learning, laughing or loving. I think Mum knew a hell of a lot about looking after our mental health before the world picked up on the trend. Thank you for creating the sense of connection with family that will always sustain me wherever I am.

INDEX

accountability 64, 89, 91, 169-171
animal brain 31–35
Arianna Huffington 106
attitudes **77**, 78–79
Asaro tribe 51

beliefs **77**, 78–79
Beyond Blue 45*n*, 101,191, 192
Brené Brown 51, 58, *64*, *70*, 166,
    204–205, 210

Centre for Creative Leadership 134
Charles Duhigg 117
classroom inside your head 30–31, 46,
    64–66, 100, 110–111, 115, 154, 198
connecting to/with self 45, **46**, 51, **94**,
    103, 120, 199
connecting with others 45, **47**, 51, **103**,
    127, 199
contribution 45, **46**, 47–50, 85, **86**, **88**,
    103, 109, 164, 207

cortisol 32–33, 38, 48–49, 59, 62-66, 122,
    132, 174, 180–181, 188–189
crisis 29, 74, 172–174, 190, 192, 205
culture 72, 76–77, 82, 92
curiosity 45, **47**, 51, 85, **86**, **88**, **103**, 148,
    152, 155, 163, 166, 171

Daniel Siegel 111, 150
Dare to Lead 205, *210*
David Pearl 166
deep breathing 121, 122–125
Deloitte 15
Derek Sivers 89
dopamine 34–37, **38**, 47, 54, 58, 68, 112,
    122, 149, 153, 156, 165, 201, 205
Drew Dudley 60

Elizabeth Kubler-Ross 185
energy assessment 98
energy level **25**, **98**, 99, 101, 125

executive brain 31, 35, 36–37, 44
exercise **108**
exponential growth 9–11, 12

Fabulous Nobodies Theatre Company 71
Faethm 11
feedback model, (see SBI Feedback
Model)
flow 112–113
food **107**
fourth industrial revolution 11, 213

Game of Thrones 210
Gandhi 214
Good to Great 128
Gratitude 115–116

habit 117–120, 133
Harvard Business Review 44
Harvard Medical School 39n, 115, 128n
Harvard Study of Adult Development 44
Henry Ford 120
heroes 77, 79–81
Hugh van Cuylenburg 12

Inside Out 30

Jim Collins 128
John C. Maxwell 129
journaling 195–199, 206

lag indicator 99–100, 102, 116
leadership 3–8, 13, 15, 21, 48, 60, 77,
89–90, 113, 129, 130–131, 134, 146, 172,
203, 208
lead indicator 97, 102, 124
laughter 60–61, 122, 202
Lifeline 29n, 190n
Lord of the Rings 213

Maslow's hierarchy 41, **42, 43**
mental health continuum (also psychological health continuum) 23–26, **27**, 28,
52, 91, 94, 124,175–181, 183–184, 192
mental health pie 45, **46**, 48-49, 85,
102–**103**, 195–197, 210

mental ill health 2–3, 12, 23, 108,
178–179
mental illness 12, 14, 23–26, **27**, 28, 108,
178, 183
Mental Health Commission of Canada
23n
mentally healthy workplace 83–85, **86**,
93, **160**, 195
Michael Priddis 11
Mihaly Csikszentmihalyi 112
mindfulness 110–112, 115
Mindsight 111, 150, 156n
MOMs (Meeting of the Minds), 114, 219
music 122
Musical Director 71, 76, 91, 166, 195

Oxytocin 33, 34–37, **38**, 47, 207

pattern-seeking 35–36, 47, 56, 127,
performance management 173, 178–179
perspective taking 115
physical health continuum **25**
psychological health continuum (See
mental health continuum)
physical self 96, 105–109
psychological self 96, 105–110

Ray Kurzweil 9n
Rising Strong 51, 58n, 64n, 70n
rituals 77, 79–81, 83
Robert Burton 58

sawubona 128
SBI Feedback Model 134–143, 147, 154,
167, 175–176
serotonin 34, **38**, 47, 112, 127, 132, 149,
156, 207
shadow talk 66, 73, 75, 85, 90, 95,
stories and story-telling 166–168
Susan David 39, 65, 128, 166

The Future of Work 15n
The Power of Habit 117
The Resilience Project 12
The Seven Habits of Highly Effective
People 55n

Waitress 45
Tony Robbins, (*Anthony*) 206
tribal, tribalism 13–14, 33

Unlimited Power 206n
Up in the Air 109

Values **77**, 77, 78, 80–81
vulnerability 7, 18, 41, 146, 149, 168, 187

World Health Organization (WHO) 2
Writing 40, 116, 121, 122–123, 168, 197,
    98–199

your Board 200–207
your shadow 54–63, 128, 133